God, Up Close and Personal

God, Up Close and Personal

A glimpse into the heart and character of God

Gwenn McKone

Publishing services by Selah Publishing Group, LLC, Tennessee. The views expressed or implied in this work do not necessarily reflect those of Selah Publishing Group.

ISBN: 978-1-58930-245-7
Library of Congress Control Number: 2010900055

Worthy of Note

All scripture quoted in this book comes from the New American Standard Bible.

◆

When quoting scripture, and the word "LORD" is in all capitals, this has been directly copied from the New American Standard Bible, and refers to God's special or proper name which is translated from the four letters "YHWH." Although God has many names in the Bible, this particular name is considered so sacred that the ancient Jews did not pronounce it. Therefore it has been consistently translated LORD (all capitals and the first capital larger).

◆

When you find quoted scripture with some words in **bold** in this book, it is because I wish to emphasize those words. It is my emphasis only, not something found in the New American Standard Bible.

◆

Also, while this book focuses on getting to know God's character, it should be noted that there is only one way to come to the Lord God—to be with Him in heaven for eternity—and that is by accepting His Son, Jesus Christ, as Lord and Savior. Jesus said, *"I am the way, and the truth and the life; no one comes to the Father, but through Me." (John 14:6)* There is simply no other way to God. Accept no substitutes.

—Gwenn McKone

*To Him Who gave me the gift of writing,
and with it, purpose and joy and meaning.
Thank you, Father God, for bringing this book to life.
May it glorify and honor You.
I love you.*

Acknowledgements

I would first like to thank my husband, Robin, who has always had an unwavering belief in me as a writer, and has encouraged me more than anyone else.

Thank you also to our two daughters, Christian and Jillian, who have always been my biggest cheerleaders. Nobody, and I mean nobody, can make me feel as important and needed as you two.

I would also like to acknowledge my wonderful Bible study group ladies at Evergreen Christian Fellowship who have prayed over me, my family, and this book for years, especially Bettye, Kim, Annegret, Kathy and Penny. Your prayers have wrought wonders in my life.

Thank you to Noma who gladly read every word of the first draft of this book as I wrote each chapter. Your wonderful comments, critiques and encouragement helped me to stay the course.

Thank you to Terry, my dearest friend, who has put up with me, loved me, and most of all, *listened* to me rant and rave for more than 35 years. You have given me that rare kind of friendship you only find once in a lifetime.

And last, but not least, thank you to my mom, Vicky, who introduced me to Jesus Christ a long time ago. If not for you, this book may not have come into existence. I hope you can read this from heaven, Mom.

Contents

I permitted Myself to be sought by those
who did not ask for Me;
I permitted Myself to be found by those who did not seek Me.
I said, 'Here am I, here am I,'
To a nation which did not call on My name.

Isaiah 65:1

Introduction

When we are born, we come equipped with a large amount of trust. Newborns are not afraid of being dropped, falling, being thrown up in the air, making a scene in public—or even of being naked in front of everyone. Babies come with an assumption that all will be as safe and warm and comfortable on the outside of the womb as on the inside.

But as we progress through life, things begin to erode our trust; things like child abuse, divorce, disease, crime, terrorism, and even things that aren't quite so dramatic such as insensitivity, insincerity, unkindness and disloyalty. Nearly all of us have trust issues to some degree. And it's no wonder. Our world is rife with issues that chip away at our trust, whether that trust is in God, parents, a spouse or friends.

As our trust is eroded, it is often replaced with things like fear, mistrust, anger and anxiety. In fact, anxiety disorders are the most common mental illness in the U.S., with 40 million (18.1%) of the adult U.S. population (age 18 and older) affected.[1]

---

[1]Statistics and Facts About Anxiety Disorders, 2009, Anxiety Disorders Association of America, 27 December 2009,< http://www.adaa.org/AboutADAA/PressRoom/Stats&Facts.asp>.

Often, our biggest trust issues are with the Lord God Himself. Why would He let bad things happen to good people? How can we release ourselves to truly trust Him with our lives, our loved ones, and our eternity?

When bad things happen to God people

It isn't easy, even for the seasoned Christian who has a close and dynamic relationship with God, because everyone knows at least one, wonderful, God-loving person whose life was marked by undeserved tragedy. It may even be our own. Because we can't reconcile the tragedy in our minds, we question God's integrity, goodness and love, and sometimes we even harden our hearts so that we can't be hurt again. Although He would like to soften and heal our offended hearts, we hold our hearts away from Him, and we remain wounded.

While we may never know on this side of heaven why such things happen, the only way we can progress beyond these tragedies to healing is to trust God, His goodness and His sovereignty. Easy to say, hard to do.

How, then, do we learn to trust Him? We learn to trust Him in the same way that we learn to trust others—over time as we observe His character. However, because God is not before us in human form, *we* have to seek to know Him. If we do not seek to know God, He will remain a shadowy figure, misunderstood and frightening, like Boo Radley in *To Kill a Mockingbird*.

Unlike Boo Radley, God has not avoided discovery. God has willingly and lovingly revealed His character to us through the Bible. The Bible was written through many centuries by many different writers. Of course, that was by God's design, because if so many different writers in different ages came up with the same impression, then we can be assured that His character is consistent, and that their observations are correct. More importantly, if we see through the Bible that His character is good, then we can begin to release ourselves to trust Him. Learning to trust in God is the most important thing you will ever do, because there will come a time when He will be the only rock you can cling to when a disaster or frightening diagnosis threatens to drown you in fear.

Let me tell you about Esther, who had cancer. She was a friend of my dear friend Joey. Although I never met Esther, Joey told me a lot about her, and asked me to pray for her on a regular basis. I came to feel like I knew Esther. She was a woman who really loved God, and trusted Him. God would do small things in her life to give her a smile and let her know He was walking with her.

Joey would send me updates on Esther's condition, which seemed stable for a few years, but then began to plunge downhill. Eventually she was in the hospital having to sit upright simply to breathe.

When Esther died in her mid-forties, I spent several weeks chewing on the whole thing, wondering why God would take such a wonderful Christian woman so early in life; why He wouldn't reach down and heal her; why He would even let cancer invade her body in the first place.

God reminded me that His perspective is from the topside, and ours is from the underside. We see the world as we know it, and think of it as beautiful; He sees the world as a tawdry caricature of its original magnificence. We see heaven as something we're told is wonderful, but somewhat frightening because we cannot see it. He sees heaven as the *real* reality, and life in the world as "seeing in a mirror dimly." We are the baby who thinks of the womb as the world, when the real world is waiting outside. So while we grieve Esther's early departure—and may even resent God for it—Esther is in fact running unencumbered and with boundless energy through breathtaking beauty, and into the arms of her Prince.

Of course, we must *trust* that this is the case for Esther, since she hasn't sent us a postcard: *"Having a great time…you should see this place! Wish you were here!"* But you know what? We *do* have a postcard of sorts. God *has* provided us with a description.

A postcard from heaven

While in exile on the island of Patmos in the Aegean sea, John the apostle was taken to heaven for the express purpose of describing it for us so that we would know and believe. What he saw in heaven is what the book of Revelation is all about.

> After these things I looked, and behold, a door standing open in heaven, and the first voice which I had heard, like the sound of a trumpet speaking with me, said, "Come up here, and I will show you what must take place after these things."
>
> Immediately I was in the Spirit, and behold, a throne was standing in heaven, and One sitting on the throne. And He who was sitting was like a jasper stone and a sardius in appearance; and there was a rainbow around the throne, like an emerald in appearance.
>
> REVELATION 4:1-3

A real God, a real throne, and an actual door into heaven. And John saw it with his own eyes. Then God gave him a glimpse of the new heaven that is to come.

> And he carried me away in the Spirit to a great and high mountain, and showed me the holy city, Jerusalem, coming down out of heaven from God, having the glory of God. Her brilliance was like a very costly stone, as a stone of crystal-clear jasper.
>
> And he showed me a river of the water of life, clear as crystal, coming from the throne of God and of the Lamb in the middle of its street. And on either side of the river was the tree of life, bearing twelve kinds of fruit, yielding its fruit every month...
>
> REVELATION 21: 10-11, 22:1-2

God leaves little to our imaginations, because He wants us to know, to believe, to *trust*. Throughout His word, He has revealed Himself, His character and even His dwelling place to us—the same place where Esther is right now.

Esther and the frog

Let's go back to the story about Esther. As I said earlier, God in his infinite tenderness would show Himself in small ways to her. Joey once told me a story about the time she and Esther went into a grocery store to pick up a few items. They went their own ways, and ended up meeting in the freezer section. They were chatting, and suddenly Esther spied a stuffed frog sitting atop some frozen vegetables. She pointed it out to Joey, and Joey opened the glass door and retrieved it. It turned out to be a little hand puppet, and when Joey stuck her hand inside the puppet, she realized it played a song. She pushed the button and the song that played was, "You are so beautiful to me." Here was Esther, bald from chemotherapy, feeling as ugly and warty as a frog, and God was delivering a message to her, "You are so beautiful to Me."

You see, God had placed that frog there for Esther to find. It was actually right around Valentine's Day, and they would find out a few minutes later that a whole box of those same frogs were for sale at the front of the store. Would she have picked up one of twenty in a box? Maybe. Maybe not. But it was the incongruity of a frog in the freezer that made Esther take notice, and allowed God to speak to her in His own inimitable way.

The story goes on. Later that day, Esther called Joey to say that she'd remembered FROG used as an acronym for "Fully Rely On God." But of course. God knew that and brought it to Esther's mind. Joey went back and got that frog for Esther, and it was in Esther's hospital room the day she died. So was God. He was up close, not at arm's distance. In fact, He was carrying her.

> Listen to me, O house of Jacob,
> And all the remnant of the house of Israel,
> You who have been borne by Me from birth,
> And have been carried from the womb;
> Even to your old age, I shall be the same,
> And even to your graying years I shall bear you!
> I have done it, and I shall carry you;
> And I shall bear you, and I shall deliver you.
> Isaiah 46:3-4

God delivered Esther personally to heaven. He opened the door for her and escorted her in. God is just as near to us, and He wants us to draw near to Him. We are His children.

> Let us therefore draw near with confidence to the throne of grace, that we may receive mercy and may find grace to help in time of need.
> HEBREWS 4:16

Let's get to know Him up close and personal, so that we can finally say, "OK, Father God, whatever You allow into my life, whether good or bad, I will trust You because You are absolutely trustworthy."

Chapter 1

Our Tender God

And the earth was formless and void, and darkness was over the surface of the deep; and the Spirit of God was moving over the surface of the waters.
GENESIS 1:2

In the beginning, the earth was like a human egg before it is given life. Imagine it. God was moving over the surface of the waters, hovering, thinking, excited, expectant. Like an artist who regards a blank canvas or a writer who begins with a blank page, His magnificent mind must have been working furiously in a kind of creative bliss, seeing in His mind's eye what wonders His words would bring into existence.

Then He shaped the earth simply by speaking. For five days, He described what should be, and it was so. For five days, He deliberately kept His hands behind His back, endowing it with its beauty and its riches with only the words from His mouth. And at the end of each day, when He regarded what He had done, "He saw that it was good."

Imagine the colors and the textures at the end of those five days—every plant, flower, fruit and bird; every rocky outcropping, towering tree, glassy lake and majestic peak in brilliant color—every detail crisp, every hue vibrant. Fragrance emanated like a halo from that new earth. Lilacs, roses and honeysuckle cast their bouquets lavishly upon the breeze to intermingle with lavender and rosemary and thyme. In other climes the sultry smell of wet dark earth and clay met tangy ocean spray. The sea creatures were frolicking in their new watercolor world, and the birds of the air were testing out their new wings.

Then came the sixth day, when He created the animals that would live on land.

> Then God said, "Let the earth bring forth living crea-
> tures after their kind: cattle and creeping things and
> beasts of the earth after their kind"; and it was so.
> GENESIS 1:24

Again, "God saw that it was good."

The Lord God had finished creating the heavens and the earth, and all that were in them simply by speaking them into existence.

We are handmade

But now He was going to create His beloved Adam and Eve, and words alone simply wouldn't do. He intended to create them with His own hands, because these would be His very own children. Just as we couldn't possibly give birth and not want to touch and caress our new baby, so, too, God wanted to hold and touch and tenderly shape His first children. He wanted them to know that they were different from the rest of His creation. More special. More beloved. His ultimate masterpiece.

So when it came time to form that first human, God took dust from the ground and formed Adam with exquisite intricacy. He personally molded His first child, gently shaping his eyes, nose and mouth, and chiseling a broad, smooth forehead and strong jaw. Surely He smiled when Adam's face took shape, and gazed for a long moment at this beautiful creature whose genes would influence the faces of the rest of humanity.

Why did God make man out of dust? It was actually loose earth, and since it was "new" loose earth, God scooped up thick, rich earth abundant in minerals and teaming with tiny organisms. That earth may even have had a red cast to it, for Adam's name means "red" or "ground." Still, it was dirt, but God is God, and He can make something amazing out of something very simple.

When He was done, God looked at his creation and saw that he was magnificent. Yet Adam was lifeless—a life-size Ken doll, so to speak. Even then, God didn't speak a word to bring him to life.

> Then the LORD God formed man of dust from the ground, and breathed into his nostrils the breath of life; and man became a living being.
> GENESIS 2:7

The first love scene

Adam and Eve were created in the image and likeness of God (Genesis 1:26). The word "likeness" in Hebrew is "D^emûwth," and it means likeness, resemblance, similitude; image, model, pattern, shape. Adam, therefore, resembled God. Although we like to ascribe a spirit form to God—and indeed, God's Holy Spirit is spirit—God also has hands that molded Adam and Eve, and lungs that breathed life into Adam. So I imagine God got onto His knees, bent over him and breathed His strong, pure breath into His new child, and brought him to life. Or perhaps He lifted Adam into His strong arms and cradled Him as He brought him to life. Either way, Adam was blessed with God's loving, physical touch.

I like to think that God actually brought His lips to Adam's in a kiss with that first breath. Although scripture says that He breathed into Adam's nostrils, the word "nostrils" is derived from the Hebrew word "Aph," which means, "the breathing part of the body, specifically the nose, nostril or face."[1] Since the mouth is also a breathing part of the body, couldn't it have been a kiss that God placed on Adam's lips as He gave him life? Isn't that how we express our love even today?

---

[1]Lexical Aids to the Old Testament. Zodhiates, Spiros, executive editor. Hebrew-Greek Keyword Study Bible. Chattanooga, TN: AMG Publishers, 1984 and 1990.

There is also a subtle yet wonderful truth here. God didn't blow His breath into the cattle or any of the animals to bring them to life, for their source of life was the earth:

> Then God said, "Let the earth bring forth living crea-tures after their [literally "its"] kind; cattle and creeping things and beasts of the earth after their [its] kind"; and it was so.
> GENESIS 1:24

The earth "brought forth" living creatures. It's not clear how that happened, but the earth brought forth its "own kind." The creatures came from the earth, and began breathing on their own, without assistance.

However, Adam's source of life was God. He was God's child, and therefore God had to bring him to life. Although Adam was indeed made from the elements of the earth, He could only become a living being with the breath of God. And with that first, lovely, pure breath of God, every succeeding human being would be a descendant of God, for God gave Adam life.

Nearly every newborn gets a slap on the bottom to induce them to take a big enough breath of air to inflate their lungs for the first time. But our tender God preferred to inflate Adam's lungs with His own strong breath and perhaps the gentle touch of His lips, while Adam rested in the comfort of His arms. Can you imagine what Adam saw when he first opened his eyes and looked upon the face of God? Can you picture the love emanating from those majestic eyes, and the delight in His smile?

The love scene between Adam and God must have been unutter-ably tender and poignant. God knew that His beloved would soon choose to sin, and He would have to separate Himself from him, so His time of intimacy with His first child was unbearably short. This must have been like giving birth to a baby and falling madly in love on first sight, then having to hand him over to an adoptive mother. *This* is heart rending, and God is not immune.

Then the Lord God did something else with His hands: He planted a garden where He planned for Adam to live. This He could have spoken into existence as well, but this was to be the most beautiful garden ever created on earth—an actual replica of a garden in heaven—and the habitation of His beloved Adam, so He planted it Himself (Genesis 2:8).

Father-son bonding

He then turned His attention to the animals.

> And out of the ground the LORD God formed every beast of the field and every bird of the sky, and brought them to the man to see what he would call them; and whatever a man called a living creature, that was its name.
>
> GENESIS 2:19

The Lord God could have—and by all rights should have—given the animals names, for He was their creator. But He gave Adam the opportunity to do so because He loved Adam and wanted him to be a part of the plan, to use his magnificent brain, and to have an influence over the future of the world.

This must have been a wonderful bonding time with God and His child. I don't think this occurred in a day. God had to bring every beast and bird to Adam, and they probably discussed each one's attributes before it was given a name.

"This one, Father, makes me smile," Adam might have said, as his eyes fell upon the little creature with a duck-like bill and an otter-like body. "It must have a name that makes people smile, too. How about...platypus?"

And how God must have chuckled and said, "Yes, I agree, Adam. Well done."

Eve, made completely from Adam

God then created Eve, but not in the same way that He created Adam. It was still very hands-on, but this time, He wanted Eve to be created from something different than dust. She would be wholly and completely made from Adam:

> And the LORD God fashioned into a woman the rib which He had taken from the man, and brought her to the man.
> GENESIS 2:22

Why didn't God make Eve from the same dust that He made Adam? Here's what *Believer's Bible Commentary* has to say:

> His bride was formed from one of his ribs, taken from his side as he slept. So from Christ's side His bride was secured as He shed His life's blood in untold agony. Woman was taken not from Adam's head to dominate him, nor from his feet to be trodden down, but from under his arm to be protected, and from near his heart to be loved.[2]

When God finished creating Adam and Eve, He stood back and surveyed it all, and this time, it was more than good. It was *very good.*

> And God saw all that He had made, and behold, it was very good.
> GENESIS 1:31A

The world, as it came into being day by day, was "good" in God's eyes. But when He saw His two beloved children in the midst of His marvelous creation, He couldn't help but break from His modesty. "Look!" He said. "Now it is *very* good," in the same way that a father

---

[2]MacDonald, William. Farstad, Art, ed. Believer's Bible Commentary. Farstad, Nashville, TN: Thomas Nelson Publishers, 1995.

looks tenderly at his children when they are sleeping and thinks to himself, "How beautiful they are, more beautiful than anything else in the world, and oh, how I love them!"

Who knows how long it took before the serpent tempted Eve, and Eve fell for it? Perhaps there was a honeymoon period, when the earth, and Adam and Eve were perfect, and God walked and talked with them in the garden. Days, weeks, months? All the Bible tells us is that they heard the sound of God walking in the garden.

From bliss, to this

After Eve was deceived by the serpent, and she and Adam ate from the tree, they suddenly felt the need to sew fig leaves to clothe themselves. The first sin resulted in the first sense of shame and fear—and the need to hide. God knew what had transpired, and came looking for them. He wanted to show them that He would pursue them always, like the Hound of heaven, because they mattered to Him. He also knew that with sin comes a reluctance to look to our Creator. So He came to them.

When He looked upon Adam and Eve, clothed in their rudimentary leaf-and-grass outfits (picture your child's first attempt at sewing), He knew He needed to clothe them properly. He made garments of leather for His sinful children, and clothed them. This was not because God was fashion-conscious. God intentionally killed an animal because a blood sacrifice was required to pay for Adam and Eve's sin.

That innocent animal was the first death on planet earth. Here was God's brand new, sparkling creation, and already, death had tarnished it. And don't overlook the pain that must have pierced God's heart as He killed that first animal, which He loved. Imagine killing your beloved family dog, because you needed to atone for your children's sin.

God could have made Adam and Eve designer outfits from natural fibers and spared the animal. But God never does anything that is not deliberate, necessary and with far-reaching implications for the coming ages. Sin always involves death and requires atonement (payment), but God always has a plan of redemption. That first blood sacrifice paid for Adam and Eve's sin, and signified the need for the ultimate blood sacrifice, Jesus Christ.

God and His beloved Son knew as they created the world together that man would fall and need a Savior. With that first sin, God began pointing to His coming Son, and through the ensuing thousands of years until Jesus was born in Bethlehem, God would continue, with His marvelous and comforting consistency, to foretell through scripture the Divine Sacrifice who would ultimately cover the sins of the world.

But that's the tenderness of God. Even after His first children traded immortality for mortality, and gave up a life of close communion with their creator, God still loved them—enough to ask His Son to die for them.

In fact, long before God created the world, He knew that Adam and Eve would sin when He placed them in the Garden of Eden. As a loving Father, He wanted to give them the choice to obey Him or not. He gave them free will. Had they chosen not to sin, they would have had a much happier ending.

You see, there were actually two very significant trees in the Garden of Eden. There was the tree of the knowledge of good and evil—Eve's downfall. There was also the "tree of life" whose fruit was never tasted. It guaranteed immortality. Had Adam and Eve eaten from the "tree of life" first, they would have lived forever.

When Adam and Eve chose to disobey God, He drove them from the garden, and posted a mighty angel at its entrance, so they could never again enter. God did not want them eating from the tree of life and thereby becoming immortal after sin had entered the picture. This would have forced them to live forever in bodies that were subject to sickness and degeneration. Once they sinned, it was then necessary for them to die, so that they could be given their eternal bodies afterward. Now *this* is mercy.

Our tender God among us again

Although sin has separated us from our heavenly Father, His devotion is unchanged, because even in Revelation, God talks about how we will, once again, be together with Him.

> And I heard a loud voice from the throne, saying, "Behold, the tabernacle of God is among men, and He shall dwell among them, and they shall be His people, and God Himself shall be among them, and He shall wipe every tear from their eyes…"
>
> Revelation 21:3-4a

Isn't it interesting that God said *twice* that He, Himself shall be among us? There's almost a tone of excitement in those words, as though He is saying, "I can't wait to be with you again!"

I believe it's all He has ever wanted…to be among us, to love us as only He can, to be the one who wipes every tear from our eyes. Sin has separated us so that we cannot see Him or feel Him, but one day, we will gaze upon Him as Adam did, and we will run into the arms of our tender God.

Chapter 2

Our Faithful God

Know therefore that the LORD your God, He is God, the faithful God, who keeps His covenant and His lovingkindness to a thousandth generation with those who love Him and keep His commandments…

DEUTERONOMY 7:9

In my life, the faithfulness of God often goes hand-in-hand with the timing of God. Over and over again, He has proven His faithfulness to me through His exquisite timing. When I'm questioning Him, or wondering if He's there, or coming to the end of my rope, He always comes through for me at specific and significant times and dates.

I know why this is the case—for me—anyway. Subtlety does not work well for my personality type. I need the proverbial brick-on-the-head. If He did not come through at specific times and dates, I might not be completely sure that it was He who was answering my prayer and I would not give Him His well-deserved praise and glory.

Let me illustrate. When I was pregnant for the second time, I was thrilled with the timing. There would have been about three-and-a-half years between the two children. But soon I began to miscarry, and I was angry with God. I even found some Bible verses that supported my belief that God would heal me and all would be well. But eventually I did miscarry, and I lamented to God, not only about the loss of the child, but about the fact that He had overlooked the wonderful timing of that pregnancy. I didn't know when I'd get pregnant again—and because I was nearly 40—I didn't have time on my side.

But there were other events happening in my life before I miscarried, and God knew I could only handle so much. My mother had informed me that she had lung cancer on the same day that I found out about my pregnancy.

I flew with my two-year-old daughter from our home in Washington to my mom and dad's home in Arizona after my mother had a few weeks to digest the news of her disease. My father had Parkinson's disease at the time and though he was fairly young, dementia accompanied the Parkinson's, so my mother had been trying to handle the challenges of his disease along with settling into the realization of her own.

My daughter and I stayed for three weeks. Unbeknownst to me until I had been there a week, I was to be the rock upon which my mother's waves of anger and fury would lash, as she waged war against her disease. After three weeks of trying to deal with her, my father and my toddler, I returned home broken. It was only a matter of a few weeks before I miscarried. I was angry with God and I was angry with my mother—sure that both had caused the loss of the baby.

God's perfect timing

But God was faithful and had an amazing plan with incredible timing. I got pregnant again within about five months, and was expecting in November. I was able to travel back down to be with my mother on Mother's Day, and then to fly back down again a few weeks later, when she was in a coma, shortly before her death. My mother passed away in May, when I was about four months pregnant.

Had I continued with the previous pregnancy, I would have been due in May—the same month my mother died. I would not have been able to be with her when she passed, or to help my brother with dissolving their estate and holding an estate sale, or to bring my father up with me to Washington and get him settled into an assisted living facility. God knew that I needed to be in top shape and unencumbered with a new baby during that time, and had every intention of blessing me with a beautiful child. With the next pregnancy, I was in my middle trimester when all these events occurred—that wonderful "feel good" stage in pregnancy—so I was able to do all that was necessary to deal with my mother's death.

But here's the real kicker: guess when that baby was born? *On her sister's birthday.* She wasn't induced. God held that child in my womb until November 16, because He was saying to me in clear, capital letters, "What were you saying about perfect timing between the children? Rely on my timing, because it is ever, and always, PERFECT!" Two children, born on the same day, four years apart. That is *so* God. He is so faithful.

One could say that the entire Bible illustrates that God's faithfulness coincides with His perfect timing. The Israelites, however, would have begged to differ. When God brought them out of Egypt via the parting of the Red Sea, He ensured that it took 40 years to reach the promised land. Never mind the fact that it was only eleven days' journey to Canaan—the promised land—from Egypt.

A spiritual cleansing

What the Israelites didn't realize for many years is that their journey to the promised land was far less a journey of distance, and far more a journey of spirit. Many of the Israelites never made it out of their own spiritual wilderness, and died there. Their eyes never beheld the promised land. God kept them in the wilderness until the older generation died, so that the promised land wasn't tainted with their disobedience, idol worship and ungratefulness.

Nonetheless, throughout their sojourn, God provided their basic necessities. When the Israelites left Egypt, they had only the clothing and necessities they could carry, and their clothing and shoes never wore out during those 40 years. While this was clearly a miracle, it was also a spiritual cleansing. They had come from Egypt, the epicenter of fashion, and even though they had spent their time there as slaves to the Egyptians, they had no doubt coveted the lifestyle.

The ancient Egyptians loved ornamentation, and all forms of jewelry, including necklaces, rings, anklets and bracelets were popular fashion accessories. Designed, crafted and worn with great thought and care, jewelry was valued not only for its beauty and precious metals, but also for the magical and spiritual protection it was thought to give the wearer.[1]

When Moses told them to leave Egypt, he directed them to first request gold, silver and articles of clothing from the well-to-do Egyptians. God had granted them favor with the Egyptians, so the Egyptians readily handed them over. In fact, the Bible says they didn't just get a few nice things, they "plundered" them. This was to fulfill God's promise to Abraham that after the Israelites had served the Egyptians for four hundred years, "... *I will also judge the nation whom they will serve; and afterward they will come out with many possessions." (Genesis 15:14)*

After God sent nine destructive (yet highly imaginative) plagues upon the land of Egypt to convince Pharoah to let His people go, the Egyptians were more than happy to heap jewelry and clothing on them to get them to leave.

So as they fled, the Israelites were loaded down with ancient Egypt's version of sequined evening gowns and designer jewelry, but few provisions. They had no idea they would be tramping through a dry and desolate land for years, and should have plundered the army surplus store instead. What they found out years later was that they needed nothing but the clothes on their back and their faithful God, for He ensured that their clothes never wore out, and their shoes never needed new soles, for all of their 40 years in the desert. When they had no water, God gushed it out of a rock. When they ran out of food, God rained manna (a fine flake-like substance, literally bread from heaven) every morning, and provided birds as meat every evening.

Manna, again?

The Israelites ate from that same menu for 40 years, and from their perspective, God had taken them out to the wilderness to torture them. From God's perspective, however, they had been in Egypt for way too long, and had learned to think like the Egyptians. In their minds,

---

[1]Fashion and style: dress and costume. 2009. Egyptology Online. 23 December 2009. < http://egyptologyonline.com/dress.htm>.

everybody who was anybody had an idol or two on their mantle, even God's chosen people. And they didn't think it was any big deal to worship them occasionally, just in case Baal and Asherah really did exist.

God needed to take them out to the wilderness and down to absolute basics to purge them and their minds of a lifestyle and belief system that, if not completely purified, would corrupt the Israelite nation. They were the only people on earth who knew God, and could tell the rest of the world about Him. While the Israelites were in captivity in Egypt for 400 years, God and His covenant with Abraham had already become fuzzy in their minds.

If the Israelites continued to let other gods infiltrate their traditions and loyalty to God, or if they left God entirely, who, then, would be God's spokespeople to the rest of the world? Who, then, would be the salt of the earth, to keep it from the kind of corruption that motivated God to cause the Great Flood? And if there was no longer a people chosen by God, representing God, and worshipping God only, from what nation, then, would Jesus, the Messiah be born? Certainly not one that spurned God, and yet every other nation on earth did that, except the Israelites. Clearly it was imperative that God purge and purify His people, even if it took 40 years to do it.

In the beginning, God's demands were few. For example, God told Moses to tell the people to gather only enough manna for one day. He did this so that they would learn to trust that He would provide for their needs the next day and the next and the next. Those who didn't trust Him gathered too much, and the next day, found worms in their manna. And those who didn't gather in the morning came out to find that it had melted away. Talk about no shelf life.

God also told them to gather extra manna only on the day before the Sabbath, so that they would not have to gather on the day of rest...and because God didn't want them to gather on the Sabbath, they did not have worms in their manna on the Sabbath, even though it had been held over for a day. Those who did not gather enough and went out to look for it on the Sabbath came up empty-handed. Not surprisingly, there were a lot of people who didn't follow God's instructions.

> Then the LORD said to Moses, "How long do you refuse
> to keep My commandments and My instructions?"
> EXODUS 16:28

Starting from square one

God had His work cut out for Him in teaching His people to listen to Him and trust Him. Little did they know that the long list of laws which God later gave to Moses while they were still in the wilderness, occurring first in the book of Exodus, occupying most of Leviticus and spilling over into Numbers and Deuteronomy, would make these first instructions seem like child's play.

There's a pattern that emerges throughout the Exodus story:

a. The people grumbled and complained
b. God came through for them
c. They soon forgot how God came through for them and when it got tough again...
d. The people grumbled and complained

Never mind the fact that they had a clear sign of His faithfulness before them as a pillar of cloud by day, and a pillar of fire by night for years. It had become like wallpaper to them. Even with a 24-hour, unearthly, miraculous, *visible* sign of God's presence burning brightly in their midst, it was only three months after the Israelites left Egypt that they committed the heinous sin of creating a golden calf to worship.

A meeting with God

Contrary to popular belief, Moses didn't make just one trip up to the top of Mount Sinai to bring down the Ten Commandments in his hands. Moses went up several times, and returned to report what God had told him. After some intimate meetings with God, God told Moses to get the people ready to meet Him, because He was going to come down on Mount Sinai in the sight of all the people. He required that they consecrate (cleanse) themselves for two days in preparation for meeting their most holy God.

> So it came about on the third day, when it was morning, that there were thunder and lightning flashes and a thick cloud upon the mountain, and a very loud trumpet sound, so that all the people who were in the camp trembled.
>
> And Moses brought the people out of the camp to meet God, and they stood at the foot of the mountain.
>
> Now Mount Sinai was all in smoke because the LORD descended on it in fire; and its smoke ascended like the smoke of a furnace, and the whole mountain quaked violently.
>
> When the sound of the trumpet grew louder and louder, Moses spoke and God answered him with thunder.
>
> EXODUS 19:16-19

As if the cloud and pillar of fire were not enough, they got to *meet* God, to see signs of His magnificence, to thrill at the sound of the blaring trumpet announcing His entrance, to tremble at the sound of His voice, to feel the earth actually quaking. Even though God had been annoyed at His people for their grumbling and disbelief, He still remained faithful, and provided them with a display of His awesome power and majesty that no one had seen before, and few have seen since.

What's even more astounding is that God spoke to them *from heaven*. While no one knows how close heaven is, it's evident that God never left His throne and yet His voice came through loud and clear. No wonder the earth quaked.

> "I am the LORD your God, who brought you out of the land of Egypt, out of the house of slavery.
>
> "You shall have no other gods before Me.
>
> "You shall not make for yourself an idol, or any likeness of what is in heaven above or on the earth beneath or in the water under the earth."
>
> EXODUS 20:2-4

While the Israelites must have been excited to meet God, they ended up experiencing holy and unmitigated terror as His booming voice shook them to the core. Like the tsunami in Indonesia in 2004, one moment they were enjoying a sunny day in the desert, and the next moment, the sky was covered by a thick, ominous black cloud while lightning flashed around them. And because God's presence is a consuming fire, the top of the mountain crackled with white-hot flames as huge plumes of smoke billowed into the sky.

The holy violence of it swept over them and nearly killed them. All they could do was cup their hands over their ears, close their eyes, and hope they would survive it. God's voice was so earth shattering, and, in fact, *ear shattering*, that afterward, the people begged Moses to ask God not to speak directly to them anymore. The Israelites thought that if God went on much longer, they would surely die.

This is not the only way that God speaks to His people. God spoke to the prophet Elijah in the sound of a gentle blowing (1 Kings 19:12). But these were a stubborn and obstinate people, and God wanted the fear of Him to remain with them long after, so that they would not sin.

By the time God finished his oratory, most of the Israelites had vacated their front-row seats. The Bible says they stood at a distance trembling. Yet the cloud of His presence remained, and Moses alone was brave enough to approach God to see if there was more to come.

> Then the LORD said to Moses, "Thus you shall say to the sons of Israel, 'You yourselves have seen that I have spoken to you from heaven.
>
> 'You shall not make other gods besides Me; gods of silver or gods of gold, you shall not make for yourselves.'"
>
> EXODUS 20:22-23

God knew that the Israelites were about to do exactly that, so He instructed Moses to reiterate His second commandment to them again. This wasn't the first time God would try to save His people from themselves (remember Eden?), and it certainly wouldn't be the last.

He already knew that they would transgress, but at least in hindsight, they would see that He had given them guidance, and not let them sin unknowingly.

The ten commandments were actually the first of many laws that God would give to Moses in the ensuing months—laws against every imaginable sin. Not only did God know what depths humanity could plumb in its depravity, He was also completely blunt and to the point about it all. He left no stone unturned, and if you think God didn't cover a potential sin, I dare you to find it missing in Exodus, Leviticus, Numbers or Deuteronomy. When God draws the line in the sand, He draws it thick and in neon-colored paint. When we choose to cross it, there is no way we can say we didn't know.

After Moses delivered God's message to the people, they reaffirmed their covenant with Him. *"All that the LORD has spoken we will do, and we will be obedient!" (Exodus 24:7b)* And they probably said it in all sincerity, little realizing that idol worship ran as deep in their culture as it does today in ours. One of the definitions of "idol" is "an object of extreme devotion." The key word here is "object." The Israelites were accustomed to having something to fix their gaze upon. Since leaving Egypt, they had fixed their gaze upon Moses.

When Moses began to spend more time on the mountain with God than with them, the Israelites grew edgy. Then God told Moses to bring up Aaron, Nadab, Abihu—the other celebrities of the sojourn—and seventy of the elders of Israel to see Him. Now not only was their esteemed leader absent, but their elders headed up into the clouds as well.

While the Israelites paced and chewed on their fingernails, the seventy elders were getting a taste of the divine—literally. They were beholding God Himself—not a cloud, as the Israelites had seen, *but Him!* And so like God, He provided food for them, because the Bible says they ate and drank. Can you imagine the banquet when God is host?

All those who gazed upon Him should have fallen down dead at the sight, since earthly beings are not able to see God and live, but God *"did not stretch out His hand against the nobles of the sons of Israel,"* (Ex. 24:11) meaning that through sheer grace He enabled them to see Him without being harmed.

God did all of this to turn the gaze of the Israelites away from the seduction of Egypt back to the pure and beautiful One Who loved them with an everlasting love. He was wooing them back, impressing them with His power and might, proving His faithfulness with His daily provision, and romancing them with His love.

Sadly, it wasn't enough for them, for their faith had not been placed in God, but in Moses. When Aaron and the elders returned from visiting with God, Moses stayed with God for 40 more days. Where was their leader? What was taking so long? They went to Aaron.

> "Come, make us a god who will go before us; as for this Moses, the man who brought us up from the land of Egypt, we do not know what has become of him."
> Exodus 32:1b

They believed that Moses had brought them up from the land of Egypt, not God. Although Moses had no power or authority apart from God, as far as the Israelites were concerned, he was the big guy with the magic staff that parted the waters of the Red Sea and brought water out of the rock. It didn't matter that the Israelites had heard all of the commandments straight from the mouth of God, and that Aaron and the elders had actually seen God, and eaten with Him. Only a few weeks after the elders' heavenly encounter, the Israelites were gathering the gold that the Egyptians had given them and melting it down to form an idol, and Aaron was spearheading the effort.

You can take an Israelite out of Egypt...

Aaron and the elders probably tried to tell the people what they had seen of God, but there were an estimated 1.5 million Israelites to their 73, and the herd mentality was clearly at work. It was all too easy—and perhaps even comforting—to revert to the idolatrous life-style they'd recently been evicted from.

Can you imagine a born and bred New Yorker being placed in the middle of Death Valley? And I'm not even talking a planned move (not that anyone would plan to move to Death Valley). I'm talking a here's-your-plane-ticket, grab-your-toothbrush-and-your-cell-phone kind of move. As soon as that New Yorker arrived in all that beautiful desolation, he'd start to get the shakes for all the space around him, and then when he couldn't find a Starbucks or a Thai restaurant, he'd be screaming for mercy. The same was true for the Israelites, and it would take some time for them to adjust to their new minimalistic, God-centered lifestyle.

> Then all the people tore off the gold rings which were in their ears, and brought them to Aaron.
>
> And he took this from their hand, and fashioned it with a graving tool, and made it into a molten calf; and they said, "This is your god, O Israel, who brought you up from the land of Egypt."
>
> Now when Aaron saw this, he built an altar before it; and Aaron made a proclamation and said, "Tomorrow shall be a feast to the LORD."
> EXODUS 32:3-5

We're talking Aaron here—the guy who saw God only weeks before. He was probably thinking that if he didn't respond to the people, he would face bodily harm. Moses had had a similar problem earlier when they had come to Rephidim and there was no water. Moses went to God and said he needed water quick, because the people were ready to stone him.

The fact that Aaron proclaimed a feast to the Lord was a weak attempt to try to turn their focus back toward the Lord, and some commentaries say they were worshipping the Lord by means of the calf. This is no excuse for their behavior, particularly in light of the fact that they chose a cow, of all things, to represent the Lord God Almighty.

When God saw what the Israelites were creating out of the gold, He told Moses what they were doing:

> "Now then let Me alone, that My anger may burn against them, and that I may destroy them; and I will make of you a great nation."
> EXODUS 32:10

Lest you think He was just threatening, consider the Great Flood, and the fate of Sodom and Gomorrah.

Moses immediately began to intercede for the people. He reminded God about His covenant with Abraham, and that it was the Israelites whom He'd said would inherit the promised land. He reminded Him about His promise of faithfulness to His people. Because God is a covenant God—a promise-keeping God—He changed His mind.

Unprepared for the shock

Moses had been quick to intercede for the Israelites while he was up on the mountain with the Lord. He knew they were sinning, but he didn't have the birds-eye-view that God did. However, his countenance changed considerably when he actually saw what they were doing. When he went down the mountain with the two tablets of testimony in his hands—written by the very finger of God—and caught his first glimpse of the wild party going on in homage to the calf (think Mardi Gras on steroids), he hurled the tablets and shattered them at the foot of the mountain.

He then took the calf, burned it with fire, ground it into a fine powder, scattered it over the surface of the brook that was coming out of the mountain—their only water source—and made them drink it. This was the scriptural equivalent of washing their mouths out with soap.

Consider how long it would take to grind a large golden calf into a fine powder, even if it had been melted with fire. This was how long and how hot Moses' anger burned against them. He was determined to ensure that not only would they not be able to reconstruct the calf or any other idol with the gold, but by drinking it, it would exit from their bodies in a form that no one in their right mind would want to use.

Then Moses called Aaron to task about the whole thing, and Aaron's reply is definitely one of the Bible's greatest punch lines:

> "For they said to me, 'Make a god for us who will go before us; for this Moses, the man who brought us up from the land of Egypt, we do not know what has become of him.'
>
> "And I said to them, 'Whoever has any gold, let them tear it off.' So they gave it to me, and I threw it into the fire, and out came this calf."
>
> EXODUS 32:23-24

There Aaron was, gesturing with his hands, acting out the scene. *And like magic, out came this calf…* Even grown-ups come up with lame excuses. God made sure that Aaron's reply made it into the Bible, word for word, so we realize that all of God's people—even those who have seen Him face to face—have had moments of weakness, faithlessness, and dishonesty.

Fortunately, God loves us in spite of our failures. Later on in this book, you will see how God eventually blessed Aaron richly with a special ministry, but not before Aaron and the Israelites were disciplined for their disobedience by having to spend forty years in the desert.

God is faithful: faithful to love us, to bless us, and even to discipline us for our own ultimate good. His faithfulness in the face of the Israelites' faithlessness is astounding. His patience and grace are as tangible as the second set of stone tablets He wrote upon after Moses lost his temper and broke the first set. Even after they had flaunted their sins before Him, God renewed His covenant with Israel. It was His promise to bless them and bring them into the promised land if they followed His commandments.

And this was only Exodus, the earth's early years. God's patience with His people had yet to be tried for thousands of years afterward. As the Bible continued to be written, He continued to prove faithful, committed, and undeterred in being a patient Father to His beloved children.

Chapter 3

Our Detail-Oriented God

"Then you shall make a lampstand of pure gold. The lampstand and its base and its shaft are to be made of hammered work; its cups, its bulbs and its flowers shall be of one piece with it.

"And six branches shall go out from its sides; three branches of the lampstand from its one side, and three branches of the lampstand from its other side.

"Three cups shall be shaped like almond blossoms in the one branch, a bulb and a flower, and three cups shaped like almond blossoms in the other branch, a bulb and a flower—so for six branches going out from the lampstand; and in the lampstand four cups shaped like almond blossoms, its bulbs and its flowers."

EXODUS 25:31-34

Our God loves to deal with details. Nothing is too small to escape His notice. The scripture above is a small portion of the expansive and meticulous directions God gave Moses for building the Tabernacle. Why? Because God cares about the details—*every detail*—and He wants to be involved in the intimate details of your life.

Some of my friends have told me that they feel weird asking God to help them with small things—things they think He is too big or too busy to be concerned with. On the contrary, God loves to be asked for

His help and advice, just as a parent would. And, let me submit that in any given neighborhood, probably only a precious few are putting Him first in their lives—so you can imagine how He revels in helping those who do.

God's detail orientation is aptly illustrated in Exodus, Leviticus and Numbers as He spells out His many laws for His people, as well as His instructions for the building of the Tabernacle, the priests' garments and the ark of the covenant. You can open those books at nearly any page and read His exacting requirements. For example:

> "And you shall make holy garments for Aaron your brother, for glory and for beauty.
> "And you shall speak to all the skillful persons whom I have endowed with the spirit of wisdom, that they make Aaron's garments to consecrate him, that he may minister as priest to Me."
> EXODUS 28:2-3

Let me interject something quickly here, slightly off-topic, but worthy of note. Remember Aaron, who molded the golden calf? God is now making him a priest. This is the special ministry that God gave to him, and *this* is God's sheer grace.

Now back to God's divine details:

> "And these are the garments which they shall make: a breastpiece and an ephod and a robe and a tunic of checkered work, a turban and a sash, and they shall make holy garments for Aaron your brother and his sons, that he may minister as priest to Me.
> "And they shall take the gold and the blue and the purple and the scarlet material and the fine linen.
> "They shall also make the ephod of gold, of blue and purple and scarlet material and fine twisted linen, the work of the skillful workman.
> "It shall have two shoulder pieces joined to its two ends, that it may be joined.

"And the skillfully woven band, which is on it, shall be like its workmanship, of the same material: of gold, of blue and purple and scarlet material and fine twisted linen.

"And you shall take two onyx stones and engrave on them the names of the sons of Israel, six of their names on the one stone, and the names of the remaining six on the other stone, according to their birth.

"As a jeweler engraves a signet, you shall engrave the two stones according to the names of the sons of Israel; you shall set them in filigree settings of gold.

"And you shall put the two stones on the shoulder pieces of the ephod, as stones of memorial for the sons of Israel, and Aaron shall bear their names before the LORD on his two shoulders for a memorial.

"And you shall make filigree settings of gold, and two chains of pure gold; you shall make them of twisted cordage work, and you shall put the corded chains on the filigree settings."

EXODUS 28:4-14

This is a very small portion of the very detailed descriptions God provided Moses. He left little to Moses' imagination. Even in regard to the engraving, He said, *"As a jeweler engraves a signet…"* And He didn't just ask him to make two chains, He specified, *"you shall make them of twisted cordage work."*

A glimpse into the mind of God

God is not only a perfectionist, but every detail He insists upon has specific meaning and symbolism. Like the Garden of Eden, God wanted to connect earth with heaven, and as Eden had once been a place where He dwelled with Adam and Eve, so, too, the Tabernacle would be a place where He would dwell with His people. Throughout history, God has tried to give us a taste of heaven on earth.

The specifications for the Tabernacle are fascinating if read in the light of God's amazing attention to detail. More than just long lists of instructions, they are a glimpse into the mind of God. For example, He takes pleasure in beauty: "*And you shall make holy garments for Aaron your brother, for glory and for beauty.*" The priest's garments were to be a reflection of God, and therefore, they needed to be of the highest quality and the utmost beauty. His taste in fabric and furnishings are clearly opulent.

Did you note the ephod, robe and tunic of "checkered work"? This wasn't referring to color, but rather that the linen should be woven into a checkered pattern. *He cared even about the actual weaving of the cloth.* Linen was a costly and highly prized fabric in those days, and God wanted His representatives to wear only the finest. While there is symbolism attached to every detail, it's not clear why God preferred that particular pattern for the fabric.

Are you getting this, Moses?

God spoke all of these requirements to Moses, word for word. Can you picture Moses taking dictation on the mountain? The laws God gave him, and the Tabernacle's specifications go on for pages and pages in three different books of the Bible. That is why Moses spent so much time on the mountain. God quite possibly could have written everything down Himself to ensure nothing was omitted. We know for certain that the ten commandments were written on the stone tablets by "the finger of God."

When David decided to build the temple, so that God would have a more permanent "house" rather than the tabernacle, God again gave him His detailed requirements. He was so deliberate about them, He penned them in His own majestic hand:

"*All this,*" said David, "*the LORD made me understand in writing by His hand upon me, all the details of this pattern.*" (*1 Chronicles 28:19*)

The Expositor's Bible Commentary explains it in this way:

> Because the words "he gave me understanding" have no "and" before them in the Hebrew but are connected with the first part of the verse rather than its latter part, we should preferably read: "the LORD gave me

understanding in writing." David was saying that not only were the temple plans revealed by God (v. 12), but that they were given to him in written form from God, to be handed to Solomon (v. 11) an ultimate testimony to their divine character.[1]

This was the equivalent of a hand-written love letter from God. He was saying, in essence, "Build this, and I will meet you there." Imagine holding an actual document containing His handwriting—an invitation to meet with Him. If we are awed by the penmanship on the Declaration of Independence, would we not be brought to our knees at the sight of a document written by God?

While we don't have that document in any museum, still, His signature is everywhere—everywhere in the uniqueness of creation. It is in our fingerprints, our DNA, our voice. God delights in making everyone and everything slightly different, and knows every intricate detail of our universe. Every hair on our head is numbered (Luke 12:7). Every star in the sky is counted and named (Psalm 147:4). A sparrow does not fall to the ground without the Father knowing it (Matthew 10:29). He knows the inner workings of our bodies, every thought that crosses our minds, and every moment of every day of our lives before we are even born. The most beautiful rendering of this is in Psalm 139:

> O LORD, Thou hast searched me and known me,
> Thou dost know when I sit down and when I rise up;
> Thou dost understand my thought from afar.
> Thou dost scrutinize my path and my lying down,
> And art intimately acquainted with all my ways.
> Even before there is a word on my tongue,
> Behold, O LORD, Thou dost know it all.
> Thou hast enclosed me behind and before,
> And laid Thy hand upon me.

---

[1]Barker, Kenneth L. and John R. Kohlenberger III. The Expositor's Bible Commentary, Abridged Edition, Old Testament. Grand Rapids, MI: Zondervan, 1994.

Such knowledge is too wonderful for me;
It is too high, I cannot attain to it.
Where can I go from Thy Spirit?
Or where can I flee from Thy presence?
If I ascend to heaven, Thou art there;
If I make my bed in Sheol, [the abode of the dead]
behold, Thou art there.
If I take the wings of the dawn,
If I dwell in the remotest part of the sea,
Even there Thy hand will lead me,
And thy right hand will lay hold of me.
. . .
My frame was not hidden from Thee,
When I was made in secret,
And skillfully wrought in the depths of the earth.
Thine eyes have seen my unformed substance;
And in Thy book they were all written,
The days that were ordained for me,
When as yet there was not one of them.

PSALMS 139: 1-10, 15-16

God knows our thoughts and our dreams. He knows *and cares* about everything. You know that little sin you haven't been talking to Him about? You might as well, because He knows. You know that topic that's kind of embarrassing to admit to God? Fess up, because He knows. You know that problem with spending, eating, drinking, smoking, gossiping, gambling, anger, anxiety, fear, swearing, pornography, sexual addiction? Talk to Him about it. He knows; of course He knows.

I have found that as I've grown closer to God, it becomes easier and easier to talk to Him about everything, and I do mean everything. Once I get it out onto the table, I realize that I don't feel condemned or embarrassed in front of Him, I just feel relieved to get it out in the open. Once it's out in the open, I know that I've given it to Him, and in so doing, I've given Him permission to deal with it. If I keep hiding it from Him, I'm just letting it fester. And pretending like the problem does not exist only makes it harder for Him to help me to overcome it.

God's detail orientation also manifests itself in His personal love language. If you are open to it, God will communicate with you in a personal love language that only He and you will understand. Let me illustrate.

A friend of mine has a son who was serving in Iraq. Her son's mission was very dangerous, and he was often in convoys that experienced mines exploding. He had seen more than one comrade killed this way. My friend was very worried about her son, and prayed a lot about it.

One day, she walked out to her garage and found a little metal toy soldier on the floor. If you're familiar with the little soldier sets that boys play with—which at one time were metal but are now made of plastic—you know that different soldiers have different functions. The soldier that she found was holding a mine sweeper.

My friend had no young children, and no idea where this toy soldier had come from—especially an old metal one—but as she examined it, she knew that it had been put there by God. He was telling her in effect that He was sending a mine sweeper ahead of her son, to keep him safe. That's one example of God's love language.

Fast forward a few months after my friend's discovery of the toy soldier. I had previously moved my 90-year-old grandmother out of her home and into an assisted living community. It was now time to fly back down and clean out her home, and do an estate sale so that it could be sold. Due to a number of deaths in my family, I was her only living relative. It was up to me to get the job done.

I was not looking forward to the task, because I was leaving my husband to watch our daughters, and I was enlisting the help of some old friends (bless them!) who lived near my grandmother's home to help me. The task seemed overwhelming. On top of it all, as soon as I arrived to proceed with cleaning out her house, I came down with the stomach flu. I was miserable, but I had to keep going because the estate sale was already advertised, my friends were only available then, and my flight could not be changed.

As I was cleaning out one of my grandmother's cupboards, I was amazed to find one, lone, metal toy soldier. This one was not a mine sweeper, but rather a guard, who carried a rifle over his shoulder. Grandma had no reason to have a metal toy soldier. There had been no little boys in her home for at least 45 years. When I saw that toy soldier, I knew immediately Who had placed it there. He was telling me, in essence, "I'm here, and I appreciate what you are doing for your grandmother. I've got your back. Hang in there. I love you."

Of course, had I not heard my friend's story, this little metal toy soldier would have held no significance. But only God and I knew what that toy soldier meant, and it was His way of communicating with me. That toy soldier spoke to me more eloquently than anything anyone could have said to me, and I still carry it in my purse.

I'm sure Esther felt the same with the stuffed green frog that sings "You Are So Beautiful to Me" in the freezer section. God is so into the details, that He plans amazing ways to communicate His love to us. The author and Bible study teacher Beth Moore recently described how, while in the hospital for surgery, the two nurses assigned to her were named Grace and Mercy. You can bet that brought a smile to Beth's face, and told her that her detail-oriented God was right by her side.

Our intimate, personal God is all over the small stuff. Bless His name.

Chapter 4

Our God Who Demands Respect

Do not be deceived, God is not mocked; for whatever
a man sows, this he will also reap.

GALATIANS 6:7

After reading a few chapters on the more warm and
fuzzy character traits of God, it might be a little jarring to come upon
this chapter. But it's important to realize that God is God and we are
mere mortals. He is the God who created the heavens and the earth;
the God who uses the earth as His footstool. He is so mighty, so all-
encompassing, we can't even begin to fathom His greatness.

When God describes Himself, He has to do so in human terms,
so that we can get a grasp, however feeble, of how big and awesome
He really is:

> Thus says the LORD,
> "Heaven is My throne and the earth is My footstool,
> Where then is a house you could build for Me?
> And where is a place that I may rest?
> "For My hand made all these things,
> Thus all these things came into being," declares the LORD.
> ISAIAH 66:1-2A

It is He who sits above the vault of the earth,
And its inhabitants are like grasshoppers,
Who stretches out the heavens like a curtain
And spreads them out like a tent to dwell in.
He it is who reduces rulers to nothing,
Who makes the judges of the earth meaningless.
Scarcely have they been planted,
Scarcely have they been sown,
Scarcely has their stock taken root in the earth,
But He merely blows on them, and they wither,
And the storm carries them away like stubble.
"To whom then will you liken Me
That I should be his equal?" says the Holy One.
ISAIAH 40:22-25

There is no equal. When He says we are like grasshoppers, He's trying to give us a sense of perspective. If God were human, we would be grasshoppers. But in reality, even that comparison is off balance. He should have made the comparison more like fleas on an elephant.

Nonetheless, according to the Bible, this huge God knows when a sparrow falls to the ground. Think about all the sparrows that live in your neighborhood. All the sparrows that live in your city. All the sparrows that live in your state, your country, your world. And we're just talking about sparrows. He knows every animal, every tiny insect, every sea creature. He also knows every person intimately.

Have you every gone to a concert or a sports event attended by tens of thousands of people, and looked around and realized that God knows every single person there, and loves them? And we're just talking about our planet. He knows what's happening moment-to-moment on every other planet and star as well. How? Because He is everywhere at all times. His Spirit permeates the universe.

It's mind-boggling. It's incomprehensible. And it should be humbling.

Under the heavy hand of God

Because God is God, He deserves and demands respect. I have no problem with this. As far as I'm concerned, it just gives Him more hero status. I certainly would not want to worship a God who allows people—grasshoppers—to treat him like a doormat. We are here by His grace, and His grace alone. Every breath we take, every move we make is allowed by sheer grace.

When David wrote the following psalm, he had committed a grievous sin. God had rebuked and chastened him, and David was thoroughly convicted of his wrongdoing. He had broken out with festering wounds over his body, had a high fever and was wracked with pain. (See Psalm 38.) He had no strength left. One commentary says this was a result of "divine wrath." Perhaps, or perhaps it was his mental anguish that was causing the physical manifestations.

The key point here is that David, a man after God's own heart, understood that the last thing he should be doing was shaking his fist at God:

> I said, "I will guard my ways,
> That I may not sin with my tongue;
> I will guard my mouth as with a muzzle,
> While the wicked are in my presence."
> I was dumb and silent,
> I refrained even from good;
> And my sorrow grew worse.
> My heart was hot within me;
> While I was musing the fire burned;
> Then I spoke with my tongue:
> "LORD, make me to know my end,
> And what is the extent of my days,
> Let me know how transient I am.
> Behold, Thou hast made my days as handbreadths,
> And my lifetime as nothing in Thy sight,
> Surely every man at his best is a mere breath.
> Surely every man walks about as a phantom;
> Surely they make an uproar for nothing;

He amasses riches, and does not know who will gather
them.

Psalm 39:4-6

David was as low as he had probably ever been. In fact, in Psalm
38, it says, "...*Thine arrows have sunk deep into me, And Thy hand has
pressed down on me.*" Think about it: he felt as though God's hand was
pressed down on him. Once again, the God/bug illustration comes to
mind. But God only presses down on us when we are acting like stink
bugs and sticking our rear ends up in the air at Him. David knew he'd
better show some respect to God or he might end up on the windshield.

Believer's Bible Commentary has a wonderful paraphrase of this
same psalm:

> I was fiercely determined to keep myself from rebel-
> ling or complaining against the Lord in spite of the
> extremity of my plight. I vowed to muzzle my mouth
> as long as I was in earshot of unbelievers; I didn't want
> to give them any excuse for questioning the providence
> of God. So there I was, dumb and silent, with no outlet
> for my suppressed emotions...Lord, how long is this
> nightmare going to last? Tell me how much time I have
> left, and when it is going to run out. At best the span of
> my life is only about the width of my palm; compared
> with Your eternity, my lifetime isn't worth mentioning.
> All of us humans are as unsubstantial as vapor. We go
> through life like phantoms. We rush around in frenzied
> activity—but what does it all amount to after all? We
> spend our lives scrimping and saving, and leave it all
> behind to be enjoyed by ingrates or fools or strangers![1]

---

[1] Macdonald, William. Farstad, Art, ed. Believer's Bible Commentary. Nashville, TN: Thomas Nelson Publishers, 1995.

Choose now what kind of rebuke

And this is the result of God's rebuke upon one who loves Him, and has spent his life trying to serve Him. For those who don't take God seriously, His rebukes are often more debilitating and permanent. This is not to say that God is a vengeful God, but He most certainly is a just God. He will always render justice.

If a sin has been committed, there are two types of responses from God, depending on where you stand with Him. If you love God and have tried to live according to His laws and precepts, God will discipline you, for the furthering of your own righteousness. If a sin has been committed by someone who knowingly and intentionally spurns God—especially if it is a sin against God Himself—He will bring about retribution. It's the difference between mercy and the lack thereof. Trust me, you will want to choose to be disciplined by a loving God. It's not fun, but it's usually not deadly.

Let's consider the choices made by King Nebuchadnezzar, king of Babylon. At the time of Nebuchadnezzar's reign, Babylon was the socio-economic center of the world, so King Neb had an enormous sphere of influence. God gave him a dream which troubled him. King Neb called up every diviner, magician and astrologer in his kingdom, and expected at least one diviner to not only interpret his dream, but to actually tell him what the dream was. If no one could, all of the magicians, conjurers, sorcerers and soothsayers in the kingdom would be torn "limb from limb, and your houses will be made a rubbish heap." (Daniel 2:5) Daniel and his friends—a group of four young men who lived in the idol-encrusted palace and worshiped Almighty God—were included in the diviner crowd, because God had given them unusual knowledge and intelligence, and they had become known for their unearthly wisdom. Clearly Daniel had as much of a vested interest in the dream and its interpretation as everyone else.

Although it's not completely clear why King Neb expected someone to tell him the content of his dream, he apparently thought that anyone could make up some cockamamie interpretation to his dream. However, if someone could actually tell him what the dream was, then clearly the gods had looked favorably upon that person and that interpretation would be the right one.

Of course, none of the diviners or astrologers had received any news from the cosmos, so they were sweating bullets. They tried to talk to King Neb about how ludicrous his demand was, but King Neb stood firm. And since God had given the king the dream, He must have laughed at the game, relishing the opportunity to inform His beloved child whom He knew well, and whom He knew would call upon His name. When Daniel went to God to ask for His help, He told Daniel what the dream was, its interpretation, and the far-reaching implications which would ultimately span through the ages.

After Daniel appeared before King Neb and correctly interpreted the first dream, Nebuchadnezzar gave God a brief nod of respect by saying, "Surely your God is a God of gods and a Lord of kings and a revealer of mysteries, since you have been able to reveal this mystery."

Unswayed by an encounter with God

The brief encounter with God didn't seem to make a lasting impression, however. It wasn't long after that King Neb made an image of gold—an idol—which was 90 feet high and nine feet wide. He then proclaimed that everyone in the land should fall down and worship the image whenever they heard a certain kind of music played. He threatened the people that if they didn't fall down and worship the image, they would be thrown into a fiery furnace.

Daniel's friends Shadrach, Meshach and Abednego refused to worship the image, and were thrown into the furnace with their hands and feet tied—a furnace so big and so hot that it killed the men who threw them in. However, Shadrach, Meshach and Abednego did not burn, but rather walked around in the furnace unbound as though in the comfort of a shopping mall. And there was a fourth person who appeared in there with them—described by King Neb himself as one who had the appearance "like a son of the gods." That could have been none other than *the* only Son of *the* only true God. Wouldn't you love to know what kind of conversation they had in there?

Then Nebuchadnezzar the king was astounded and stood up in haste; he responded and said to his high officials, "Was it not three men we cast bound into the midst of the fire?" They answered and said to the king, "Certainly, O King."

He answered and said, "Look! I see four men loosed and walking about in the midst of the fire without harm, and the appearance of the fourth is like a son of the gods!"

Daniel 3:24-25

When King Neb saw that, he called the three men out. Why didn't he call the fourth man out? Did he not know how to address Him? Did he have a feeling, somewhere down in his soul, that he was gazing at the beautiful Son of the most High God and could only stare in awe? I can imagine Jesus gazing straight into Neb's eyes and leaving him startled and breathless. Whatever the actual scenario, only the three men departed the furnace and this time, King Neb gave a more formal acknowledgment of God before the peoples of the earth.

"It has seemed good to me to declare the signs and wonders which the Most High God has done for me.

"How great are His signs, And how mighty are His wonders! His kingdom is an everlasting kingdom, And His dominion is from generation to generation."

Daniel 4:2-3

King Neb experienced an astounding encounter with God. Yet like so many other people, as time passed by, the amazement he felt when he saw the miracle of the four men in the fiery furnace became fuzzy with time. Although he had acknowledged God, he still clung to his gods and still continued to build his kingdom and his wealth, with little thought for the poor and needy.

God then gave him another frightening dream. The dreams, as described in the Bible, don't seem all that frightening in and of themselves, so I imagine that because they were given by God, they must have been very real and King Neb was left shaken.

This time, Daniel interpreted the dream to mean that if King Neb didn't change his ways and show mercy to the poor, his prosperity would be cut off. In the dream, King Neb was a beautiful and flourishing tree, which was about to be cut off, with only a stump and roots left. God gave King Neb one whole year to show mercy to the poor. If he did not, he would be driven away from mankind to live "and share" with the beasts of the field, eat grass like cattle, and be drenched with the dew of heaven until seven periods of time (years) would pass over him.

God had two things He expected of the king: to acknowledge that God (and not Neb) was the supreme ruler, and to show mercy to the poor and needy in his kingdom. King Neb could choose to do so by his own initiative, or under the heavy and surprisingly swift hand of God.

> "And in that it was commanded to leave the stump with the roots of the tree, your kingdom will be assured to you after you recognize that **it is Heaven that rules.**
>
> "Therefore, O king, may my advice be pleasing to you; break away now from your sins by doing righteousness, and from your iniquities by showing mercy to the poor, in case there may be a prolonging of your prosperity."
>
> DANIEL 4:26-27

Unfortunately for King Neb, he didn't take Daniel or God seriously. Perhaps he found Daniel's predictions a little too far-fetched to swallow. The great King Nebuchadnezzar, ruler of the greatest kingdom of the world at that time, living with the beasts of the field, eating grass and drinking dew? Right…

I just love this about God—His incredible creativity—even in disciplining His people. He could have been more conventional and enabled a neighboring king to come and overthrow King Neb and put him in prison or something similar, but then, it certainly wouldn't look like a God thing. When God puts His hand to things, He makes sure that it's something only He can do, nobody else can take the credit, and the individual being chastened knows exactly who's doing the chastening.

God ALWAYS follows through

So it was exactly one year later while King Neb was strutting on the roof of the royal palace of Babylon, puffed up with pride like a peacock, that he had another close encounter with God.

> "The king reflected and said, 'Is this not Babylon the great, which I myself have built as a royal residence by the might of my power and for the glory of my majesty?'
> DANIEL 4:30

Of course God knew, with His exquisite timing, that King Neb would be congratulating himself exactly one year after he heard David's interpretation and warning.

> "While the word was in the king's mouth, a voice came from heaven, saying, 'King Nebuchadnezzar, to you it is declared: sovereignty has been removed from you, and you will be driven away from mankind, and your dwelling place will be with the beasts of the field. You will be given grass to eat like cattle, and seven periods of time will pass over you, until you recognize that the Most High is ruler over the realm of mankind, and bestows it on whomever He wishes.'
> "Immediately the word concerning Nebuchad-nezzar was fulfilled; and he was driven away from mankind and began eating grass like cattle, and his

body was drenched with the dew of heaven, until
his hair had grown like eagles' feathers and his nails
like birds' claws.

DANIEL 4:31-33

BAM. Just like that. No arguments. No negotiations. King Neb
was drenched, eating grass and growing feathers. Some commentaries
attribute this description to King Neb becoming temporarily insane.
Others say he thought he was a beast, referring to "boanthropy," a rare
form of mental disorder which makes a person think they are a cow.
One commentary suggests that the ancients often regarded insane
people as "possessed" by a god, and therefore the king may have been
kept in a park and given deferential treatment.[2] But the Bible says he
was driven away from mankind.

Nebuchadnezzar actually could have turned into a beast. There is
no hair, no matter how matted and messy, that looks like feathers. And
if he was driven away from mankind, this does not sound like a kind
and discreet sequestering by his nobles. He was simply driven away,
either as cattle are driven, or via a heavenly vehicle, just as Philip was
transported during the early church:

> "And when they came up out of the water, the Spirit
> of the Lord snatched Philip away; and the eunuch saw
> him no more, but went on his way rejoicing.
> "But Philip found himself at Azotus; and as he
> passed through he kept preaching the gospel to all the
> cities, until he came to Caesarea."
> ACTS 8:39-40

Philip was "snatched away" and "found himself" at Azotus. One
moment he was on the road between Jerusalem and Gaza, and the
next moment, he was in Azotus—many miles away. Nebuchadnezzar
probably had a similar experience, and found himself in a very remote

---

[2]Pfeiffer, Charles F., Everett F. Harrison, eds. The Wycliffe Bible Commentary.
Chicago, IL: Moody Press, 1962.

place, living among the wild donkeys (Daniel 5:21). Scripture refers to him as having the "heart" of a beast—and that could be interpreted as his mind. Whether he thought he was a beast or actually was one is really of no consequence. The point is, God is not mocked, and when Nebuchadnezzar would not take God seriously and pursue righteousness, God humbled him swiftly and surely. King Nebuchadnezzar finally got the point. God gave him seven long years to preen his feathers and think about it. When God restored him to his former self, King Neb made a proclamation.

> At that time, my reason returned to me. And my majesty and splendor were restored to me for the glory of my kingdom, and my counselors and my nobles began seeking me out; so I was reestablished in my sovereignty, and surpassing greatness was added to me.
>
> Now I Nebuchadnezzar praise, exalt, and honor the King of heaven, for all His works are true and His ways just, and **He is able to humble those who walk in pride**.
>
> Daniel 4:36-37

Oh yeah. He's able, all right. That is the end of King Neb's story; the Bible does not record him getting in trouble with God again. Unfortunately, however, pompousness and pride ran in the genes, and his grandson, Belshazzar, apparently didn't heed the stories he heard from his grandfather.

Belshazzar thumbs his nose at God

When Belshazzar was king, he held a huge feast for a thousand of his nobles.

> When Belshazzar tasted the wine, he gave orders to bring the gold and silver vessels which Nebuchadnezzar his father [the term "father" was also used for

grandfather] had taken out of the temple which was
in Jerusalem, in order that the king and his nobles,
his wives and his concubines might drink from them.

Then they brought the gold vessels that had been
taken out of the temple, **the house of God** which was
in Jerusalem; and the king and his nobles, his wives,
and his concubines drank from them.

They drank the wine and praised the gods of
gold and silver, of bronze, iron, wood, and stone.

DANIEL 5:2-4

Every time I read the sentence above, I cringe. I can already begin
to feel the pressure of God's hand upon the foolish king.

Suddenly the fingers of a man's hand emerged and
began writing opposite the lampstand on the plaster
of the wall of the king's palace, and the king saw the
back of the hand that did the writing.

DANIEL 5:5

Is this great or what? God's creativity at work again here. This is
by far my favorite account of God showing Himself as the God Who
is not mocked. This is better than Hollywood. This is just so God.

Then the king's face grew pale, and his thoughts
alarmed him; and his hip joints went slack, and his
knees began knocking together.

DANIEL 5:6

You bet Belshazzar's knees were knocking. When it says his hip
joints went slack, it means he could barely stand up. Can you imagine? A hand—just a hand—writing on the wall. That would freak
anyone out.

The king called aloud to bring in the conjurers, the
Chaldeans [a people noted for their astrologers], and
the diviners. The king spoke and said to the wise men

of Babylon, "Any man who can read this inscription and explain its interpretation to me will be clothed with purple, and have a necklace of gold around his neck, and have authority as third ruler in the kingdom."
DANIEL 5:7

The inscription was apparently written in a language or a script that only God knew, and probably because he wanted only one man to interpret it: Daniel. Belshazzar was frightened enough to decree something completely unheard of: that he would confer the right of kingship on the person who could interpret the writing. Belshazzar and his father, Nabonidus, were co-regents, although Nabonidus was not that interested in ruling over Babylon and moved to Tayma, a rich city in Arabia, leaving his son to rule over Babylon.

Then all the king's wise men came in, but they could not read the inscription or make known its interpretation to the king.
Then King Belshazzar was greatly alarmed, his face grew even paler, and his nobles were perplexed.
DANIEL 5:8-9

Isn't the Bible great? Don't you just love the descriptions? "His face grew even paler..." He was white as a ghost. He was also not thinking clearly, because he should have remembered who had helped his grandfather King Neb out. Fortunately, his mother the Queen came to the rescue. She told him to summon Daniel, and Daniel did not mince his words:

Then Daniel answered and said before the king, "Keep your gifts for yourself, or give your rewards to someone else; however, I will read the inscription to the king and make the interpretation known to him.
"O king, the Most High God granted sovereignty, grandeur, glory, and majesty to Nebuchadnezzar your father.

"And because of the grandeur which He bestowed on him, all the peoples, nations, and men of every language feared and trembled before him; whomever he wished he killed, and whomever he wished he spared alive; and whomever he wished he elevated, and whomever he wished he humbled.

"But when his heart was lifted up and his spirit became so proud that he behaved arrogantly, he was deposed from his royal throne, and his glory was taken away from him.

"He was also driven away from mankind, and his heart was made like that of beasts, and his dwelling place was with the wild donkeys. He was given grass to eat like cattle, and his body was drenched with the dew of heaven, until he recognized that the Most High God is ruler over the realm of mankind, and that He sets over it whomever He wishes.

"Yet you, his son, Belshazzar, have not humbled your heart, **even though you knew all this,** but you have exalted yourself against the Lord of heaven; and they have brought the vessels of His house before you, and you and your nobles, your wives and your concubines have been drinking wine from them; and you have praised the gods of silver and gold, of bronze, iron, wood and stone, which do not see, hear or understand. But the God in whose hand are your life-breath and your ways, you have not glorified.

"Then the hand was sent from Him, and this inscription was written out.

"Now this is the inscription that was written out: 'MENE, MENE, TEKEL, UPHARSIN.'

"This is the interpretation of the message: 'MENE'—God has numbered your kingdom and put an end to it.

"'TEKEL'—you have been weighed on the scales and found deficient.

"'PERES'— [UPHARSIN is the plural of PERES. The "U" means "and."] your kingdom has been divided and given over to the Medes and Persians."

Then Belshazzar gave orders, and they clothed Daniel with purple and put a necklace of gold around his neck, and issued a proclamation concerning him that he now had authority as the third ruler in the kingdom.

DANIEL 5:17-29

Here's the real kicker:

That same night Belshazzar the Chaldean king was slain.

So Darius the Mede received the kingdom at about the age of sixty-two.

DANIEL 5:30-31

God does not waste time. In fact, as Belshazzar was having his bawdy feast, the Persian army was outside Babylon's city walls. Babylon was about to fall, and the Medo-Persian empire was about to be ushered in. It would happen that very night—BAM—probably only hours later.

If you're wise, you'll take that as a lesson. If you treat God and His holy objects with anything other than the ultimate reverence, the results could be life-threatening, if not world-changing. And if God's judgment is not swift, as it was in the case of Nebuchadnezzar and Belshazzar, don't assume for a moment that God is not on top of things. If no obvious repercussions have occurred, He is either granting a time of grace, as He did with Nebuchadnezzar, or He has a different plan. But no one, and I mean no one, gets away with thumbing their nose at God.

Creative justice

God will dole out justice in His perfect timing, and according to His will. King Herod Agrippa, who killed the Apostle James and imprisoned Peter, had begun to think of himself as god-like, much like every Herod before. One day when he went to the rostrum and began delivering a message to the people, they began shouting, *"The voice of a god and not of a man!"* (Acts 12:22). Instead of correcting the people and giving glory to the only true God, he bathed in the accolades. BAM! An angel of the Lord struck him, *"and he was eaten by worms and died."*

Think on this. The angel of the Lord could have simply struck and killed him. But again, everyone would have thought that he'd simply had a heart attack. No, God had to put His unique stamp on Herod Agrippa's death, so people would know unmistakably Who had struck him down. And I really believe God has a great sense of theater, too. Do you see the order of events in his death? The worms appeared *first* and began devouring his flesh, and *then* he died, not the other way around. Death by worms. What a spectacle. I can hear the gasps resonating like a wave through the crowd. Now you know where Hollywood gets its inspiration. As Beth Moore puts it, God is the ultimate "drama King."

And here's another story, which occurred much earlier in the history of the world—during Moses' time. After seven days of a consecration ceremony making Aaron and his sons priests in the Tabernacle, they took up their official duties on the eighth day. God had given them very specific instructions as to how to offer the various offerings to Him; there was a sin offering, burnt offering, people's offering, grain offering, peace offering and wave offering. There was to be no deviation.

> Now Nadab and Abihu, the sons of Aaron, took their respective firepans, and after putting fire in them, placed incense on it and offered strange fire before the LORD, which He had not commanded them.
>
> And fire came out from the presence of the LORD and consumed them, and they died before the LORD.
>
> Then Moses said to Aaron, "It is what the LORD spoke, saying,

'By those who come near Me I will be treated as holy,
And before all the people I will be honored.'"
So Aaron, therefore, kept silent.
LEVITICUS 10:1-3

You see, God was very intentional about everything involved in the Tabernacle. He Himself had lit the first fire in the Tabernacle, and it was never allowed to go out. Therefore, every fire after that was lit from God's original fire. The "strange fire" offered by Nadab and Abihu was probably fire that was not taken off the brazen alter, as God had instructed. So, God consumed them and their strange fire with His own fire. They, unfortunately, served as examples to the rest of the Israelites about tampering with God's rules, and His holy Tabernacle. You can bet that strange fire never appeared in the Tabernacle again.

How devastating it must have been for Aaron to watch two of his sons killed instantly, but he was not about to question God after that. Even if Aaron had entertained any thoughts of objecting, Moses strictly warned Aaron and his two surviving sons, Eleazar and Ithamar, not to tear their clothes and show any sign of mourning, so that they would not make God wrathful against the whole congregation. This was no time for tirades.

BAM, down to the pit

Interestingly, tirades did become the doom of Korah, Dathan and Abiram who later rebelled against the leadership of Moses and Aaron. This time, God pulled out all the stops and split open the ground on which they stood, and then promptly closed it over them, their families and all their possessions. Essentially, everything that was connected with those men and their families went down into Sheol (the netherworld), so that when the earth closed back up, there was no evidence of them ever existing. You can bet that the earth that had split open only moments before now regained its exact former topography, without so much as a pebble out of place. *This* is divine wrath—neat, tidy, and permanent.

Those who sided with them and were still left above ground were subsequently consumed by fire. Everyone else turned tail and ran, afraid that the same fate would befall them. (See Numbers 16 for the full dramatic account.)

When you spurn God, and He knows you will not repent (this is always an option, of course), His retribution is complete and final. In another story, the Amalekites picked on the wrong people—God's people, the Israelites—and subsequently sealed their very unhappy fate:

> Then the LORD said to Moses, "Write this in a book as a memorial, and recite it to Joshua, that I will utterly blot out the memory of Amalek from under heaven."
> EXODUS 17:14

The Amalekites had attacked the Israelites as they were trying to enter Canaan, the promised land. They did so in a very underhanded way—they attacked the "weary and worn" stragglers at the rear. (Deuteronomy 25:17-19) According to *The Expositor's Bible Commentary*, "the Amalekites disappeared from history after the time of Hezekiah. Their incorrigible wickedness was such that annihilation was necessary. Besides, by their attacks on God's people, the Amalekites indicated that 'they had no fear of God.'"[3]

The Amalekites were annihilated—blotted out from under heaven. Whether the Amalekites ended up in the netherworld like Korah, Dathan and Abiram is unknown. But the fact is, they were blotted out from God's memory, and therefore, wherever they ended up, they have been eternally forgotten.

---

[3]Barker, Kenneth L. and John L. Kohlenberger III. The Expositor's Bible Commentary Abridged Edition. Grand Rapids, MI: Zondervan, 1994.

Treat God with reverence

To put it succinctly, there are three primary rules that should be earnestly followed to avoid the wrath of God:

1. Never treat God, God's sanctuary or sacred implements as anything but holy. (Using God's name as an expletive or even an exclamation, "Oh God!" or "Oh my God!" is *not* advised and actually violates the third commandment.)
2. Never infer that you or anyone or anything else are a god. All glory should be given to God and God alone.
3. Never, *ever* mess with God's children. While we are all created by God, God's children are those who love God and His beloved Son Jesus, and seek His kingdom and His righteousness.

This is the same God who lives today. He still demands respect. He still requires that we follow His laws to have life and peace. Those who are committing evil or spurning God and have not felt the pressure of His hand upon them may think they're in the clear. But God will bring them to justice, either now in this life, or the next.

'Vengeance is Mine, and retribution,
In due time their foot will slip;
For the day of their calamity is near,
And the impending things are hastening upon them.'
◆
'See now that I, I am He.
And there is no god besides Me.
It is I who put to death and give life.
I have wounded, and it is I who heal.
And there is no one who can deliver from My hand.
'Indeed, I lift up My hand to heaven,
And say, as I live forever,
If I sharpen My flashing sword,
And My hand takes hold on justice,
I will render vengeance on My adversaries,
And I will repay those who hate Me.'
Deuteronomy 32:35, 39-41

This may not be a message that anyone wants to read about our God, but make no mistake: God has a warning sign attached to Him. If you don't read it, and heed it, you're walking into dangerous territory.

Our God is an awesome God. He deserves and demands our respect and reverence.

Chapter 5

Our Jealous God

"—for you shall not worship any other god, for the
LORD, whose name is Jealous, is a jealous God—"
EXODUS 34:14

After reading the preceding chapter, it would seem that the
"jealous" aspect of God's character is equally intimidating. However,
as I hope to illustrate in this chapter, God's jealousy is for our benefit,
and if we view it that way, we'll realize that this is one kind of jealousy
that is, in fact, good.

To set the stage, you must know that God wants a specific, intense,
monotheistic, tunnel vision devotion from us. This does not mean we
can say we "believe in God" and have a Buddha in our backyard. This
also does not mean we can call ourselves Christians simply because
our parents called themselves Christians, in the same way that people
choose their political alignment because of their parents' preferences.
God made it very, very clear in his Word as to what He expects from us:

"Hear, O Israel! The LORD is our God, the LORD is one!
"And you shall love the LORD your God with all your
heart and with all your soul and with all your might."
DEUTERONOMY 6:4-5

If you really look at these words, you can derive a world of meaning from them. First of all, have you ever noticed how many times God tells His people in His Word that He is the only God? The only one. THERE ARE NO OTHER GODS, so don't even go there, not even with a seemingly innocent display of some stone or cast concrete representation of Buddha or Brahma for the sake of aesthetics. And don't think about praying to humans—even ones who've lived remarkable lives—after they've died and most likely gone to heaven. They are still humans, they are still God's children; they have not turned into lesser gods.

Love God deliberately

Once you acknowledge there is only one God, and all others are simply man-made or man-promoted, then God expects you to love Him. That is His one stringent requirement. If this is His expectation, it stands to reason, then, that loving God is not an emotion which we must somehow conjure up, but an act of will. And quite honestly, true love of anyone is an act of will. He understands that we cannot perceive Him with any of our five senses, but we must trust that He is there, and sees and hears us. That is why loving Him must be a conscious, deliberate and *daily* decision.

He wants us to put Him first in our lives, our hearts, our thoughts. He doesn't want lip service; He wants intense, intentional, committed, go-for-broke, give-it-everything-you've-got love from us. God is a lavish God, and He never asks for more than He is willing to return to us with compound interest. In today's language, what God is saying is, "Love Me with everything you've got, make Me your ultimate priority, and I will blow you away with the plans I have for you."

Why would God expect such tunnel-vision devotion from us? Doesn't that make Him a very self-serving, self-centered God? On the contrary, God knows that this world is littered with spiritual minefields and pits set by the devil himself. Some are obvious, but most are remarkably subtle. The Bible says that the devil disguises himself as an angel of light. We can be easily misled. This is how people get caught in various addictions, strongholds, destructive relationships and bad choices. The only way we can be safe from the schemes of the enemy is to keep our eyes and our devotion fixed on God, who, unlike the devil, has wonderful plans for our lives.

> 'For I know the plans that I have for you,' declares the LORD, 'plans for welfare and not for calamity to give you a future and a hope.'
> JEREMIAH 29:11

God is jealous for our future. He wants it to go according to His "plans for welfare." But if we do not fix our gaze and our devotion upon Him, we will be easily turned aside toward the "bright shiny objects" that grab our attention. The problem is, those bright shiny objects could be the devil himself—the prince of darkness clothed in shimmering light—and we won't realize it until we are up to our necks in quicksand.

If we were in heaven, worshipping and loving God would be as natural as breathing. Our God, the Author of love and grace, is the answer to our every heart's desire, and we would be drawn to Him like a moth to a flame. But here on earth, where faith without sight is the only thing that ties us to God, we must be diligent to reinforce and strengthen that tie, lest someone come along and break it.

For those who don't know God, an expectation like this from Him seems like a sacrifice—a sacrifice of our time, our priorities, our brain space. However, it's actually quite the opposite. Knowing and loving God is like entering a beautiful, enchanting world with so many levels, you can't begin to plumb its depths and farthest reaches. The further you go into His presence, the more amazed and thrilled and enchanted you become. God does not disappoint. Consider the ocean. Have we ever discovered all of its riches, and has any scuba diver ever emerged from its depths and not said, "Wow, that is incredible!"? Remember, God made the ocean and all that is in it. Imagine, then, what God is like.

> Oh, the depth of the riches both of the wisdom and
> the knowledge of God! How unsearchable are His
> judgments and unfathomable His ways!
>
> ROMANS 11:33

The rewards of loving God

God does not expect our ultimate devotion without rewarding us with His amazing love and faithfulness in return. And the wonderful thing about God is that the closer we draw to Him, the more He blesses our earthly relationships—our marriages, our relationships with our children and family members, and our friendships.

God actually made us for a two-way relationship with Him. It's in our genetic makeup. Whether we realize it or not, we were created with a deep-seated need to communicate with our creator. Some of us have learned to identify that need, and talk regularly with our marvelous and attentive God, and often hear His wise responses, if we have cultivated the right kind of hearing. Others feel that need to communicate with God, but misinterpret it, and therefore seek for a higher communion in the wrong places, and with other make-believe gods—or with the devil himself.

God also created a need in us for a perfect love, which only He can supply. All of us have at least once expected someone on earth to provide that perfect love, and we have been sorely disappointed. Some people spend their whole lives searching for that perfect love. Since new romance often masquerades as perfect love, they go from one relationship to another as soon as the other person's faults begin to show, because they can't face the truth that all people are fallible, sinful and sometimes downright rotten.

God wants to fill the need that He created within us with a personal relationship with Him. That statement alone should stop us in our tracks. *Almighty God* wants to have a personal relationship with us. He wants us to come to Him first for everything; for every pain, every need, every worry, and with words of praise for the bountiful blessings He bestows on us. He knows every minute detail about us and our lives and He is able—and more importantly, *willing*—to handle everything we bring to Him. Nothing is too small, or too inconsequential. In fact, He specializes in showing us that He cares about it all.

Those who've never sought a personal relationship with God and His son Jesus have never had the delightful opportunity of watching how God makes His presence known in the lives of those who seek Him. He delights in doing small things for us that show us that He is mindful of us. He is the supreme Lover and presents us with love gifts when we least expect it.

Who else can say "I love you" this way?

I wrote in an earlier chapter about the metal toy soldier that He left for me in my grandmother's home. Another time, I was driving through a wild, mountainous area on my way to a class at a small community college. I was tense, watching for wildlife, hoping I wouldn't hit anything. So I prayed, "Lord, it would be so nice to be able to see your lovely animals without having to worry about hitting them." Only a few minutes later, I came around a corner, and there, standing in the road, far enough ahead so that I could easily slow down, were a mother elk and her baby. I knew instantly that God had placed them there in response to my prayer. I had to smile at God's love gift.

God's love gifts are sometimes so personal, it's breathtaking. A few years ago, I was going through a very, very difficult time in my life. In fact, it was the darkest time I've ever experienced. My mother had passed away about five years earlier from lung cancer, and my father passed away four years later from Parkinson's disease. After my mother's death, I had moved my father up near me into a care facility, and had straddled the responsibilities of being a parent of two young girls, and visiting and caring for my father. I watched him deteriorate for about four years, and shed many tears in the process.

After he died, I experienced a short-term health issue which frightened me, but was dealt with successfully through surgery. After dealing with this health issue, I started to fall apart emotionally. The long-term stress finally took its toll. I couldn't eat and lost a lot of weight. I became weak and felt awful. After about three or four months of going down into what could be none other than "the pit," God spoke to me.

He kept mentioning a woman's name in my mind. This woman was someone I knew very casually. She went to my church and was in my garden club, but I really didn't know her.

Finally, after hearing her name again and again, and wondering why God was mentioning her to me, I finally gave in, and called her, feeling sheepish. She was wonderful and very open to God's leading. She told me that she had gone through the very same thing a few years before, and that's when I knew why God had directed me to her. We began meeting together and praying, and now, five years later, we are dynamic prayer partners and we have seen amazing answers to the prayers we have prayed together.

The other interesting thing about my friend is that she has an uncanny resemblance to my mother. God planned that as well. You see, my mother and I never had a good relationship. There was a lot of strife between us, even though I had longed for a loving relationship. Eventually I came to accept that it would never happen on this side of heaven. So when God brought this friend to me, He was not only giving me someone who had been through what I'd been through, but He was restoring to me what I had longed for in my mother, but never had.

My friend is only ten years older than me—not old enough to be my mother—but still, every time I see her, there's a flash of memory that flits across my brain when I'm looking at her, and I see my mother as she could have been—a friend, mentor, confidante and prayer partner. God's gifts are so personal, so tailor-made, that we know beyond a shadow of a doubt that they are from Him.

God takes His father role seriously

God's jealousy for us speaks of His devotion. While we can't directly compare our relationship with God to our human relationships, sometimes it helps to compare in this way just to get a small grasp. If you are a parent, and another child knocked your child down, how would you feel if she went to a friend to be consoled, and hugged, and to have that person put a bandage on her knee? Wouldn't you be saying, "Hey, wait a minute, I'm her mom (or her dad), and she's supposed to come to me! I know her best, and only I can console her and hug her the way she needs to be consoled, and I want to be sure that the wound is clean before the bandage is put on. That's my responsibility and I want to be the one to do it for her." Believe it or not, God feels the same way.

Time and again in the Bible, God tell us that those who seek Him will find Him. He makes Himself available to us. We are the absolute apple of His eye.

> "For the LORD's portion is His people;
> Jacob is the allotment of His inheritance.
> He found him in a desert land,
> And in the howling waste of a wilderness;
> He encircled him, He cared for him,
> He guarded him as the pupil of His eye.
> Like an eagle that stirs up its nest,
> That hovers over its young,
> He spread His wings and caught them,
> He carried them on His pinions."
> DEUTERONOMY 32: 9-11

The first line of this scripture is particularly arresting. *"For the Lord's portion is His people."* The *Matthew Henry Complete Commentary on the Whole Bible* explains it eloquently:

All the world is his. He is owner and possessor of heaven and earth, but his church is his in a peculiar manner. It is his demesne, his vineyard, his garden enclosed. He has a particular delight in it: it is the beloved of his soul, in it he walks, he dwells, it is his rest forever. He has a particular concern for it, keeps it as the apple of his eye. He has particular expectations from it, as a man has from his portion, has a much greater rent of honour, glory, and worship, from that distinguished remnant, than from all the world besides. That God should be his people's portion is easy to be accounted for, for he is their joy and felicity; but how

77

they should be his portion, who neither needs them
nor can be benefited by them, must be resolved into
the wondrous condescensions of free grace.[1]

We are His delight, His portion, His "garden enclosed," as Matthew Henry describes it. We…are…His. While jealousy is not a desirable trait for one person to have toward another, God alone is rightfully jealous because we are His possession.

And before you begin to chafe against the thought that you are a possession, let me state emphatically that being God's possession is the best possible situation we could ever fall into. God wants nothing more than to bless us richly, to give us ultimate freedom and eternal life. We are talking about a lavish, creative God who earnestly desires to delight His children:

> And the LORD of hosts will prepare a lavish banquet
> for all peoples on this mountain;
> A banquet of aged wine, choice pieces with marrow,
> And refined, aged wine.
> And on this mountain He will swallow up the
> covering which is over all peoples,
> Even the veil which is stretched over all nations.
> He will swallow up death for all time,
> And the LORD GOD will wipe tears away from
> all faces.
> And He will remove the reproach of His people
> from all the earth;
> For the LORD has spoken.
> ISAIAH 25:6-8

---

[1]Henry, Matthew. <u>Deuteronomy 32</u>. 2009. Heartlight's Search God's Word. 31 December 2009 http://www.searchgodsword.org/com/mhc-com/view.cgi?book=de&chapter=032

He jealously guards His possessions

Because we are His—those who love Him with all of our heart and soul—He zealously guards us. This is another behavior associated with jealousy, defined as "solicitous or vigilant in maintaining or guarding something," and God is passionate about protecting His people.

> The LORD will guard your going out and your coming in
> From this time forth and forever.
> PSALM 121:8

How thrilling to know that God considers us such a treasure that He would guard our every move...forever! Who would not want to be so loved and protected?

When I think about being God's possession, I get a visual of a boy I used to go to school with. He was big for his age, with red hair, large teeth, and strong, sinewy muscles. He was built "like a brick house" and looked kind of scary. His name was Randy.

When we entered junior high school, I began to experience some bullying by other girls in my grade. Randy had a kind heart—although few people knew that because he put up a very threatening front—and he and I were buddies. I soon learned to make it clear to the rest of the world who I was allied with, because nobody, and I mean *nobody* messed with Randy.

I feel the same way about God. I'm happy to be possessed by Him and I'm thrilled that He's jealous of me. When the devil starts messing with me, I stand behind Him and let Him fight my battles for me. If I were no one's possession, I would be wandering in this world with no one to guide me, no one to protect me, and fighting my battles alone.

Those who do not recognize God's possession of them are doing exactly that—trying to find their own way and fighting their battles alone—because God does not show up to fight for those who do not align themselves with Him. He's nobody's fool. He won't fight for someone who won't give Him the glory after He delivers them from the enemy, and He won't bless someone who doesn't even acknowledge Him.

Although it would seem an obvious choice, many people choose not to love God, because they are afraid they will lose their freedom, they will no longer be their own master, and they might have to stop doing some of their "favorite things"—things which may not really be so good for them. Still, He waits:

> "I permitted Myself to be sought by those who did not
> ask for Me;
>   I permitted Myself to be found by those who did
> not seek Me.
>   I said, 'Here am I, here am I,'
>   To a nation which did not call on My name."
> ISAIAH 65:1

And so He watches as thousands upon thousands seek after a counterfeit of His love, and end up broken, disappointed and in despair.

A friend of mine is married to a man 30 years her senior. He is now in his eighties. He has skirted around a relationship with God his entire life, and he now knows that the end of his life nears. He recently became afraid to go to bed at night, because he did not want to die in his sleep. He began taking antidepressants, just to calm down. Why, I wonder, at this point in his life, is he so unwilling to go to God? Perhaps he doesn't know that after all those eighty years, God is still waiting for that man to come to Him, and will still receive him with open arms.

God jealously desires our love because He does not want us to be disappointed. He made us with a God-sized hole in our hearts which only He can fill, and He doesn't want us to end up at the age of 80, afraid to go to sleep because we've chased after the wrong god.

God's jealousy is a demonstration of His great love for you. He wants you to love only Him because He is the only real thing. He is the only One who satisfies. He is the only One who delivers. He is the only One who allows you to go to sleep unafraid. Everything else is just a counterfeit.

Chapter 6

Our Heroic God

"No weapon that is formed against you shall prosper; and every tongue that accuses you in judgment you will condemn. This is the heritage of the servants of the LORD, and their vindication is from Me," declares the LORD.

ISAIAH 54:17

God is our redeemer, our protector and our supreme lover—the ultimate hero. And somewhere in the deepest recesses of our hearts, we have a vision of what our ultimate hero is like. We try to portray this vision on television and in the movies. But when the cameras stop rolling, the actors—even the biggest of heartthrobs—become mere mortals again, put their pants on one leg at a time, and wake up with serious morning breath.

> But now, thus says the LORD, your Creator, O Jacob,
> And He who formed you, O Israel,
> "Do not fear, for I have redeemed you;
> I have called you by name; you are Mine!

In my distress I called upon the LORD,
And cried to my God for help;
He heard my voice out of His temple,
And my cry for help before Him came into His ears.
Then the earth shook and quaked;
And the foundations of the mountains were trembling
And were shaken, because He was angry.
Smoke went up out of His nostrils,
And fire from His mouth devoured;
Coals were kindled by it.
He bowed the heavens also, and came down
With thick darkness under His feet.
He rode upon a cherub and flew;
And He sped upon the wings of the wind.
He made darkness His hiding place, His canopy around Him,
Darkness of waters, thick clouds of the skies.
From the brightness before Him passed His thick clouds,
Hailstones and coals of fire.
The LORD also thundered in the heavens,
And the Most High uttered His voice,
Hailstones and coals of fire.
He sent out His arrows, and scattered them,
And lightning flashes in abundance, and routed them.
Then the channels of water appeared,
And the foundations of the world were laid bare
At Your rebuke, O LORD,
At the blast of the breath of Your nostrils.
He sent from on high, He took me;
He drew me out of many waters.
He delivered me from my strong enemy,
And from those who hated me, for they were too mighty for me.
They confronted me in the day of my calamity,
But the LORD was my stay.

He brought me forth also into a broad place;
He rescued me, because He delighted in me.
The LORD has rewarded me according to my righteousness;
According to the cleanness of my hands He has rec-
ompensed me.

PSALM 18:6-20

Only one true hero

Don't you love the imagery in this Psalm? It has some great action scenes. Milenniums before Hollywood began to create heroes on cel-luloid, David (inspired by God) was writing about the only true hero, and how He will stop at nothing to rescue us. What's wonderful about this text is that though this description of God would at first glance seem to be greatly exaggerated, it is actually all supported by other portions of scripture. We know that the Israelites experienced the earth shaking and the mountains trembling, Abraham was overcome by His thick darkness, the enemies of the Gibeonites were slaughtered by His hailstones, and the citizens of Sodom were annihilated by His coals of fire. Isn't it a wonder that when His children cry for help, He springs into action, bowing the heavens to get to us?

Our heroic God also cares about the needy, and when no one steps forward to care for them, He cares for them *Himself.*

"The afflicted and needy are seeking water, but there
is none,
And their tongue is parched with thirst;
I, the LORD, will answer them Myself,
As the God of Israel I will not forsake them.
"I will open rivers on the bare heights,
And springs in the midst of the valleys;
I will make the wilderness a pool of water
And the dry land fountains of water."

ISAIAH 41:17-18

Caring for the needy is so high on God's priority list that there are numerous references to it in His word:

"Woe to you, scribes and Pharisees, hypocrites, because you devour widows' houses, even while for a pretense you make long prayers; therefore you shall receive greater condemnation."

MATTHEW 23:14

Learn to do good;
Seek justice,
Reprove the ruthless;
Defend the orphan,
Plead for the widow.

ISAIAH 1:17

You shall not oppress a hired servant who is poor and needy, whether he is one of your countrymen or one of your aliens who is in your land in your towns.

You shall give him his wages on his day before the sun sets, for he is poor and sets his heart on it; so that he may not cry against you to the LORD and it become sin in you.

You shall not pervert the justice due an alien or an orphan, nor take a widow's garment in pledge.

But you shall remember that you were a slave in Egypt, and that the LORD your God redeemed you from there; therefore I am commanding you to do this thing.

When you reap your harvest in your field and have forgotten a sheaf in the field, you shall not go back to get it; it shall be for the alien, for the orphan, and for the widow, **in order that the LORD your God may bless you in all the work of your hands.**

When you beat your olive tree, you shall not go over the boughs again; it shall be for the alien, for the orphan, and for the widow.

When you gather the grapes of your vineyard, you shall not go over it again; it shall be for the alien, for the orphan, and for the widow.

> And you shall remember that you were a slave in
> the land of Egypt; therefore I am commanding you to
> do this thing.
>
> DEUTERONOMY 24:14-15, 17-22

Heroic deeds earn great benefits

Although God our hero does not necessarily need our help to accomplish His will in helping the needy, He expects us to be His ambassadors. We were not created for a self-centered existence; we were created to love and help others.

If we take on that role, the scripture above says that He will bless us. When God says He will bless us, this does not mean He will give us the "usual." It means we will be well taken care of, and blessed beyond our expectations. If anyone knows how to bless, God does. Read on.

> "Now it shall be, if you will diligently obey the LORD
> your God, being careful to do all His commandments
> which I command you today, the LORD your God will
> set you high above all the nations of the earth.
>
> "And all these blessings shall come upon you **and
> overtake you,** if you will obey the LORD your God.
>
> "Blessed shall you be in the city, and blessed shall
> you be in the country.
>
> "Blessed shall be the offspring of your body and
> the produce of your ground and the offspring of your
> beasts, the increase of your herd, and the young of
> your flock.
>
> "Blessed shall be your basket and your kneading
> bowl.
>
> "Blessed shall you be when you come in, and
> blessed shall you be when you go out.
>
> "The LORD will cause your enemies who rise up
> against you to be defeated before you; they shall come out
> against you one way and shall flee before you seven ways.

"The LORD will command the blessing upon you in your barns and in all that you put your hand to, and He will bless you in the land which the LORD your God gives you.

"The LORD will establish you as a holy people to Himself as he swore to you, if you will keep the commandments of the LORD your God, and walk in His ways.

"So all the peoples of the earth shall see that you are called by the name of the LORD your God, and they shall be afraid of you.

"And the LORD will make you abound in prosperity, in the offspring of your body and in the offspring of your beast and in the produce of your ground, in the land which the LORD swore to your fathers to give you.

"The LORD will open for you His good storehouse, the heavens, to give rain to your land in its season and to bless all the work of your hand; and you shall lend to many nations, but you shall not borrow.

"And the LORD shall make you the head and not the tail, and you only shall be above, and you shall not be underneath, if you will listen to the commandments of the LORD your God, which I charge you today, to observe them carefully, and do not turn aside from any of the words which I command you today, to the right or to the left, to go after other gods to serve them."

DEUTERONOMY 28:1-14

I read this passage and marvel. And sometimes I smile... "You shall be the head and not the tail..." God knows how to give good gifts. Spectacular gifts, actually. And all He asks is that we follow His laws which, when boiled down, require us to serve Him and Him only; to be kind, fair, honest and generous; and to take care of the needy. This is over-simplification, but this is at the heart of God's heart.

Because God is consistent, the same yesterday, today and tomorrow, we can read this passage with confidence and know that these same laws apply to us today. This is God's economy. God will always be the champion of the needy and the downtrodden, and He will always reward those who extend a hand to them.

Recently, my grandmother died and because I was her only surviving relative, I received a sizable inheritance. I felt very blessed, and believed that I should begin giving some of that away to help others in need. One of the first things I did was to send a small check to a long-time friend of mine who has breast cancer, and is dealing with the extra costs of her treatment. I expected absolutely nothing back from God, since I felt that I had already been given a huge blessing from Him. But amazingly enough, a few weeks later, my husband told me that he had gotten an unexpected bonus, and that bonus was many, many times the amount I had given to my friend. God never stops giving, and He gives lavishly. When you give to someone in need, you can bank on the fact that God will reward you.

Hero even to the undeserving

And by the way, God is indiscriminate about those in need. Everyone has known someone who has gotten themselves into a big mess because of bad choices. And it's easy to look upon them and say, "Well, you made your bed, now you've got to lie in it." Yes, there are certain natural consequences to things we do. If we do drugs, we fry our brain and leave ourselves open to diseases like AIDS through intravenous drug use and shared needles. If we race someone through traffic, we could get ourselves or others killed. If we have multiple sex partners, we are far more likely to contract an STD, and have far-reaching emotional problems. God usually allows us to suffer a certain amount of natural consequences. We have to wallow in the mud for a while to realize we don't want to live the life of a pig.

God is more than willing to lift up those who have screwed up—and for all intents and purposes—should get their just desserts. (This should give all of us tremendous hope, I might add.) The caveat is that

He will do it at the right time, and when He feels we earnestly want to turn away from our transgressions. That's usually when we've eaten all the slop we can stomach.

There's a story in the Old Testament about a woman named Hagar who fits that description exactly. Hagar is not one of my favorite characters. In fact, I think God should have thumped her on the head. But He didn't.

Hagar was Sarah's Egyptian maid. Sarah was Abraham's wife. (Sarah was called Sarai at the time; Abraham was called Abram until God changed their names and subsequently changed their lives.) God had promised Abraham a son, and told him that through that son, the Israelite nation—God's chosen people—would come. In fact, God made a covenant with Abraham, and told him that his descendants would be as numerous as the stars.

Yet Abraham and Sarah were quite old when God told him this, and Sarah had never been able to conceive. She was long past child-bearing age. Because of this, Abraham assumed God was referring to their servant, Eliezer of Damascus, because the law stipulated that if you had no children, your personal servant would be your heir. But God said no, the child would be from Abraham's own body.

Amazing as it sounded, Abraham believed that it would happen as God said. Sarah may have believed it at first, too, however, years dragged by and still, Sarah did not become pregnant. She must have gone to Abraham more than once and said, "It's been years, Abraham. He may have said that, but maybe He meant something different."

Sarah decided to take matters into her own hands. She had begun to think that when God told Abraham that the heir would come from Abraham's own body, perhaps He meant to use another woman besides herself as the mother. So she gave her maid Hagar to Abraham and told them to get together and make a baby.

She told them to do what?!

I believe this took an enormous amount of sacrifice on Sarah's part, even if her motivations were misguided. Hagar was much younger, and while Sarah had always been beautiful, even into old age, she was handing her husband over to a younger, possibly more attractive woman. Abraham was eighty-five at the time, and Sarah was seventy-five. (Considering Abraham's age, conceiving with him might have been a sacrifice on Hagar's part as well, but who knows, they lived a lot longer then, and their eighty might have been our forty. Sarah went on to live 127 years, and Abraham 175 years. He even took another wife after Sarah died and had six more children, but that's another story.)

Back to the point. Because God had not stipulated who the mother would be (it should have been inherently obvious but Sarah and Abraham didn't think so) Abraham listened to Sarah. Of course, had Abraham really known the character of God, he would have realized that God would never have made such a promise to Abraham with a plan to use anyone other than his wife.

Hagar and Abraham did make a baby, but here's the part that makes Hagar seem like a wretch. When she found out she was pregnant, she began to flaunt it in Sarah's face.

> And he went in to Hagar, and she conceived; and when she saw that she had conceived, her mistress [Sarah] was despised in her sight.
> And Sarai said to Abram, "May the wrong done me be upon you. I gave my maid into your arms; but when she saw that she had conceived, I was despised in her sight. May the LORD judge between you and me."
> GENESIS 16:4-5

It seems to me Hagar should have taken a much humbler attitude, considering that she had committed adultery with Sarah's husband and had conceived when her mistress could not. She was a servant, and should have remembered her place. But now that she was Abraham's mistress and the mother of his child, she was sure she had moved up in status.

Now look what you've done!

Sarah reacted in typical female fashion. It was now all Abraham's fault. He should have gotten that woman under control, and now she was way more uppity than Sarah could stand. She had felt pretty self-righteous giving her husband to Hagar, and assisting God in that way. And what had she gotten out of the deal? Nothing but grief.

Abraham responded by telling Sarah to do with Hagar what she thought was best.

> But Abram said to Sarai, "Behold, your maid is in your power; do to her what is good in your sight." So Sarai treated her harshly, and she fled from her presence.
> GENESIS 16:6

I believe Abraham was appealing to Sarah's nobler side, but Sarah had selective hearing at that point. She heard, "Behold, your maid is in your power…" and that was all the ammunition she needed. She couldn't kick her out—Abraham's heir was in Hagar's womb—but she'd certainly make life hell for her in the process.

Sarah's treatment must have been pretty bad, because Hagar ran, pregnant, without a place to go. She ran into the wilderness and the angel of the Lord found her by a spring of water. This is actually considered a Christophany—the "angel of the Lord" is considered to be a preincarnate appearance of Jesus—one of several Christophanies in the Old Testament.

> Now the angel of the LORD found her by a spring of water in the wilderness, by the spring on the way to Shur.
> And he said, "Hagar, Sarai's maid, where have you come from and where are you going?" And she said, "I am fleeing from the presence of my mistress Sarai."
> Then the angel of the LORD said to her, "Return to your mistress, and submit yourself to her authority."
> Moreover, the angel of the LORD said to her, "I will greatly multiply your descendants so that they shall be too many to count."

The angel of the LORD said to her further,
"Behold, you are with child,
And you shall bear a son;
And you shall call his name Ishmael,
Because the LORD has given heed to your affliction.
"And he will be a wild donkey of a man,
His hand will be against everyone,
And everyone's hand will be against him;
And he will live to the east of all his brothers."
Then she called the name of the LORD who spoke
to her, "Thou art a God who sees"; for she said, "Have
I even remained alive here after seeing Him?"
GENESIS 16:7-13

Hagar named the well Beer-lahai-roi, which literally means "well of the One who lives and sees me." God sees. Nothing escapes Him. God had compassion on Hagar, just when she least deserved it. And just when He should have thumped her on the head, He promised that Ishmael would also be the father of many descendants. This was also because Ishmael was Abraham's son. However, because Ishmael was conceived in sin, our just God was not going to let her out easy. Ishmael was going to be a "wild donkey of a man" who did not get along with others. Hagar was going to have her hands full. He also told her to go back and submit to Sarah's authority, which was surely a bitter pill to swallow.

One little sin and one giant ripple

In addition, because Abraham and Sarah did not wait for God's perfect timing and trust Him completely, the ramifications of their sin would resonate through the ages. Ishmael would become the father of the Arab nation; Isaac, the future son of Abraham and Sarah, would be the father of the Israeli nation. To this day, the two nations are bitter enemies.

You have to give Sarah and Abraham some slack. Abraham was 75 when God first told him he would have descendants who would become a great nation. Abraham was 100 when Isaac was born to Abraham and Sarah. Twenty-five years is a long time to wait for the fulfillment of a promise.

When Isaac was born, Ishmael was about fourteen, and already his unfortunate temperament was showing. On the day that Isaac was weaned, Abraham threw a huge feast, and Ishmael began mocking them. Now the true heir of God's chosen people had been born—the people through whom God's son Jesus would emerge—and Ishmael, although still beloved by Abraham, had lost a significant amount of status in the household. Sarah had put up with Hagar and her upstart son for far too long, and enough was enough.

> Therefore she said to Abraham, "Drive out this maid and her son, for the son of this maid shall not be an heir with my son Isaac."
>
> And the matter distressed Abraham greatly because of his son [Ishmael].
>
> But God said to Abraham, "Do not be distressed because of the lad and your maid; whatever Sarah tells you, listen to her, for through Isaac your descendants shall be named.
>
> "And of the son of the maid I will make a nation also, because he is your descendant."
>
> So Abraham rose early in the morning, and took bread and a skin of water, and gave them to Hagar, putting them on her shoulder and gave her the boy, and sent her away, and she departed and wandered about in the wilderness of Beersheba.
>
> GENESIS 21: 10-14

I find it interesting that Abraham did not even make any provisions for Hagar except for bread and a skin of water. Had he no friends who could take her in? He knew exactly how long that bread and water would last her and Ishmael in the wilderness. It must have been painful sending them out and watching them go—he loved Ishmael, his son, even if he could be a donkey. But Abraham was nothing if not obedient to God, and God had told him to listen to Sarah.

I believe God knew there was room for only one woman in that home, so Abraham had better just let her clean house, if you know what I mean. Abraham also probably believed that God would provide for Hagar, in the same way that he would later believe that God would provide when He asked him to sacrifice his beloved son, Isaac.

God to the rescue

Hagar once again found herself wandering out in the wilderness, but this time, with young Ishmael. They had clearly not made friends. Sarah might have made room for Hagar and Ishmael if they'd shown some humility, and if Hagar had taught Ishmael to be a little more respectful. Yet again, God met them in their time of greatest need.

> And the water in the skin was used up, and she left the boy under one of the bushes.
>
> Then she went and sat down opposite him, about a bowshot away, for she said, "Do not let me see the boy die." And she sat opposite him, and lifted up her voice and wept.
>
> And God heard the lad crying; and the angel of God called to Hagar from heaven, and said to her, "What is the matter with you, Hagar? Do not fear, for God has heard the voice of the lad where he is.
>
> "Arise, lift up the lad, and hold him by the hand; for I will make a great nation of him."
>
> Then God opened her eyes and she saw a well of water; and she went and filled the skin with water and gave the lad a drink.
>
> And God was with the lad, and he grew; and he lived in the wilderness and became an archer.
>
> GENESIS 21:15-20

The fact that God was going to make a nation of Ishmael was not news to Hagar. He had already told her that the first time she was in the wilderness. But sometimes it can look really bleak, particularly when God doesn't come immediately to our aid. I wonder if He was waiting for Hagar to call out to Him; to tell Him that she remembered the promise He had made to her, and that she believed He would follow through.

But she didn't. She just walked away from her son, believing he would die, and not wanting to witness it. They had been in the wilderness for a while because the water had run out, and though I'm sure she pondered if God remembered His promise, it probably began to seem like a hallucination that she'd ever heard from God at all.

Fortunately, God comes to our aid even when we don't believe He will. The old saying, "God is never too early and never too late" is so true. He is our hero and loves us with an everlasting love. He sees us even when we are wandering in the wilderness, whether it's an actual wilderness, or the wilderness of our own souls.

How many of these Hagars are living around us right now? These people are God's priority, because they are the ones whose hearts are ripe, ready to receive His saving grace. They have made bad choices and are walking around in their own personal wilderness and they are thirsty and hungry for God. And He *will* save them, either by using us, His ambassadors, or by doing it Himself, just as He did with Hagar. She was alone with her son, but He was with her.

Only God is our faithful hero in this world, even when we don't deserve His grace. Only God will never leave us or forsake us. Consider the following words of our wild, heroic, fiercely protective God:

> "In righteousness you will be established;
> You will be far from oppression, for you will not fear;
> And from terror, for it will not come near you.
> "If anyone fiercely assails you it will not be from Me.
> Whoever assails you will fall because of you.
> "Behold, I Myself have created the smith who blows
> the fire of coals,
> And brings out a weapon for its work;
> And I have created the destroyer to ruin.

"No weapon that is formed against you shall prosper;
And every tongue that accuses you in judgment you
will condemn.
**This is the heritage of the servants of the LORD,
And their vindication is from Me**," declares the LORD.

ISAIAH 54:11-17

Doesn't that feel good? Doesn't it make you swoon? God, the only true hero, is always with you and will gladly defend you. You can count on it.

Chapter 7

Our Generous God

"Bring the whole tithe into the storehouse, so that there may be food in My house, and test Me now in this," says the LORD of hosts, "if I will not open for you the windows of heaven, and pour out for you a blessing until it overflows."

MALACHI 3:10

Our God wants to bless us. But He first wants us to bless Him. It's another one of those backward, upside-down, inside-out precepts of God that makes perfect sense once you think about it.

If God simply blessed us and expected nothing in return, we would assume that the blessings were just things that we had earned ourselves, or good karma, or serendipity. Furthermore, we would have no incentive to give to others, particularly those who can't give back. Sure, it's easy to give to our loved ones because we love them. But it isn't so easy to hand out our hard-earned money to nameless, faceless people lumped under the name of a particular charity, or someone on the street corner who's holding up a "homeless" sign—the same able-bodied someone who's been squatting on that corner for months.

So God says to us in essence, "Give to the orphans, the widows, the needy and all who ask for something from you, and I will reimburse you. And my reimbursement will be with interest."

This kind of giving requires faith. And trust. If you're following God's requirements to the letter, and handing money to anyone who asks, it also requires separating yourself from your personal prejudices because your money may not always be used the way you'd like it to.

For example, when you give money to a clean-cut, business-suited investment banker, you have a reasonable level of comfort that he's going to invest your money wisely. But when you hand your money to a street person, you have a reasonable amount of certainty that he's going to spend it on alcohol or drugs. And it seems like a waste of money, but it's not. It's not up to us to worry about what happens to that money when it leaves our hands. All we need to know is that we have given to God, and He will bear the responsibility for what harvest is reaped from the money in that person's life.

That's kind of freeing, don't you think? When Jesus told us to give to those who ask, He didn't place stipulations on His statement.

> "Give to him who asks of you, and do not turn away
> from him who wants to borrow from you."
> MATTHEW 5:42

We don't have to look at someone, and make a personal determination as to whether they really need what we can give them or not. We just need to give. It may not be about the money at all. That person may simply need our personal contact. The fact is, if we've given to someone with his hand out, we can know with absolute certainty that God saw us do it, and we will be rewarded.

It's easy to become jaded about the people who stand on street corners with their cardboard signs. I know I have. A few years ago, my then twelve-year-old daughter and I walked by a street bum who stuck his hand out to us. I smiled at him, shook my head and kept on walking, and after we passed, my daughter said, "Mom, I hate walking by those guys and not giving them anything. How do you know that he hasn't eaten for a few days?"

When we passed by him again, I handed him some money, and his eyes lit up, and he thanked us profusely. When we'd moved away, my daughter said, "Mom, did you see his face? He was really happy to get that." That, in and of itself, was a reward—and to know that my daughter had pelted me out of my complacency. (Kids have a tendency to expose your hypocrisy quite handily, and God will use them in that way if necessary.)

Make the first move

This is not to say that street people are the only ones we should be handing our money to…or even our first priority in giving. The point is, in God's economy, we have to make the first move and give, and believe unequivocally that God will do what He says, in His time. If you write out a check to put in the offering plate at church or for a charity, you may not see reimbursement in the next week or month. You may not even see "reimbursement" in the way that you expect. But you are guaranteed to have your needs provided for, and you will be blessed.

In the book, *God's Smuggler*, Brother Andrew talks about how he came to understand that God has a "royal way" in regard to His provision for His children. Many years ago, Brother Andrew was at a missionary training school in Scotland, where they charged no tuition, only room, board and other costs such as for soap, razors or toothpaste. Everything came to them by trusting God. *Everything*.

Brother Andrew began to realize that trusting God for everything was not an easy thing. He came to a point where he really needed to know if God was who He said He was, and if God would do what He said He would do.

> If I were going to give my life as a servant of the King, I had to know that King. What was He like? In what way could I trust Him? In the same way I trusted a set of impersonal laws? Or could I trust him as a living leader, as a very present commander in battle? The question was central. Because if he were a King in name only, I would rather go back to the chocolate factory. I

would remain a Christian, but I would know that my religion was only a set of principles, excellent and to be followed, but hardly demanding devotion.

And somehow, sitting there in the moonlight that September night in Glasgow, I knew that my probing into God's nature was going to begin with this issue of money. That night I knelt in front of the window and made a covenant with Him. "Lord," I said, "I need to know if I can trust you in practical things. I thank you for letting me earn the fees for the first semester. I ask You now to supply the rest of them. If I have to be so much as a day late in paying, I shall know that I am supposed to go back to the chocolate factory."

It was a childish prayer, petulant and demanding. But then I was still a child in the Christian life. The remarkable thing is that God honored my prayer. But not without first testing me in some rather amusing ways.[1]

God did supply his needs, and always on time.

I never mentioned the school fees to anyone, and yet the gifts always came at such a moment that I could pay them in full and on time. Nor did they ever contain more than the school costs, and—in spite of the fact that the people who were helping me did not know one another—they never came two together.

God's faithfulness I was experiencing continually, and I was also finding out something about His sense of humor.[2]

When a fellow student began asking to borrow his soap and toothpaste, Andrew gave willingly, but began to wonder what to do when God did not supply money to replenish what was being borrowed—and the borrower continued to borrow. Andrew began to

---

[1]Brother Andrew. God's Smuggler. Old Tappan, New Jersey: Fleming H. Revell Company, 1967.

[2]Ibid.

think that God was showing him the difference between a want and a need. But it did seem odd that God let him get to the point where his toothpaste tube hadn't a trace of toothpaste left in it, and he was having to sharpen his razors on his arm.

Then a real need did arise—he had to renew his visa and it cost a shilling to send it in registered mail by the end of the year. Brother Andrew didn't have even a shilling. Without the visa, he would have to leave the school.

> I did not believe that God was going to let me be thrown out of school for the lack of a shilling.
>
> And so the game moved into a new phase. I had a name for it by now. I called it the Game of the Royal Way. I had discovered that when God supplied money He did it in a kingly manner, not in some groveling way.[3]

The Royal Way

As Brother Andrew waited for God to supply the money to pay for his registered letter, he was tempted to depart from the Royal Way. He was head of the student body and in charge of the school's tract fund. It occurred to him more than once that he could borrow a shilling from the fund and pay it back as soon as possible. But he put the idea behind him.

> And then it was the twenty-ninth of December. Two days left…That morning the thought occurred to me that perhaps I might find those pennies lying on the ground.
>
> I had actually put on my coat and started down the street before I saw what I was doing. I was walking along with head bowed, eyes on the ground, searching the gutter for pennies. What kind of Royal Way was this! I straightened up and laughed out loud there on the busy street. I walked back to school with my head high, but no closer to getting the money.

---

[3]Ibid.

The last round in the game was the most subtle of all. It was December 30. I had to have my application in the mail that day if it was to get to London on the thirty-first.

At ten o'clock in the morning, one of the students shouted up the stairwell that I had a visitor. I ran down the stairs thinking that this must be my delivering angel. But when I saw who it was, my heart dropped. This visitor wasn't coming to bring me money, he was coming to ask for it. For it was Richard, a friend I had made months ago in the Patrick slums, a young man who came to the school occasionally when he just had to have cash.

With dragging feet I went outside. Richard stood on the white-pebble walkway, hands in pockets, eyes lowered. "Andrew," he said, "would you be having a little extra cash? I'm hungry."

I laughed and told him why. I told him about the soap and the razor blades, and as I spoke I saw the coin.

It lay among the pebbles, the sun glinting off it in just such a way that I could see it but not Richard. I could tell from its color that it was a shilling. Instinctively I stuck out my foot and covered the coin with my toe. Then as Richard and I talked, I reached down and picked up the coin...But even as I dropped the coin into my pocket, the battle began. That coin meant I could stay in school. I wouldn't be doing Richard a favor by giving it to him: he'd spend it on drink and be thirsty as ever in an hour.

While I was thinking up excellent arguments, I knew it was no good. How could I judge Richard when Christ told me so clearly that I must not. Furthermore, this was not the Royal Way! What right had an ambassador to hold onto money when another of the King's

children stood in front of him saying he was hungry.
I shoved my hand back into my pocket and drew out
the silver coin.

"Look, Richard," I said, "I do have this. Would it
help any?"

Richard's eyes lit up. "It would, mate." He tossed
the coin into the air and ran off down the hill. With a
light heart that told me I had done the right thing, I
turned to go back inside.

And before I reached the door the postman turned
down our walk.

In the mail of course was a letter for me. I knew
when I saw Greetje's handwriting that it would be from
the prayer group at Ringers' and that there would be
cash inside. And there was. A lot of money: A pound
and a half—thirty shillings. Far more than enough to
send my letter, buy a large box of soap, treat myself
to my favorite toothpaste—and buy Gillette Supers
instead of Blues.

The game was over. The King had done it His way.[4]

Don't settle for less than His best

God tested Andrew to see just how much He trusted Him. And
Andrew almost settled for the one measly shilling on the ground. But
God had far more blessings in store if Andrew continued along the
path of the Royal Way. I wonder: if Andrew had held onto that shilling, would that letter with the money in it have come?

I believe many people hold onto their money and don't give to
God's causes, and subsequently live with their "measly shilling" when
they could be living with thirty times that by following the Royal Way.

If you haven't figured it out by now, God is not equitable. He does
not give equally to everyone. God rewards those who diligently seek
Him and trust Him. However, the difference between the blessings

---

[4]Ibid.

given to the "seekers" and the "non-seekers" is not always easily distinguishable, because God does bless everyone on a daily basis whether they recognize it or not.

There are many people who woke up this morning with good health, a nice home and a good job. And they have been waking up like that for a long time, and have not once stopped to thank God for it. In fact, there are those who adamantly deny God's hand in their lives. Why does He bless those who don't acknowledge Him?

God blesses because He loves his children—all of His children—just as parents give things to their disrespectful and ungrateful teenagers because they love them. And perhaps He sees, somewhere in the distance, a time when an ungrateful child of His will finally want to fill that God-sized hole with Him and His love.

Seek God's favor

That said, it's important to realize that while God blesses some people, He BLESSES others. You could categorize the former as God's benevolence, and the second as God's favor. And let me tell you from personal experience, you really want to select door number two.

About a year ago, I moved my grandmother from where she was living in California at an assisted living facility up to a similar facility in Washington near me. Not long after that, I was watching Joyce Meyer talking on television about a time when she tithed more than usual to God, even though it was a financial hardship. Only about a week later, God more than reimbursed her through an unexpected check in the mail.

My husband and I decided to do the same. I kept watching the mailbox for a similar reimbursement from God, but nothing was forthcoming. I fully believed that God would come through, but He always seems to delight in doing it in ways other than I expect.

During this time, my grandmother's health was failing. A little over two months after moving her to my state, she passed away. Her death came on my birthday and about a month after I wrote that check. Upon her death, I was the sole inheritor of Grandma's estate, and with it, God's lavish response to my measly check. When I told people that my grandmother died on my birthday, everyone offered additional sympathy, but I told them that, in fact, it was God's wonderful timing.

Grandma and I had been very close for many years. I was her last surviving relative and it was up to me to make sure she received good care. When I moved her up near me, it soon became apparent that she would require much more of my time than I expected, even though she was in assisted living. I was running back and forth to be with her every few days, while also trying to be a wife, homemaker and mother to our 7- and 11-year-old girls. It was also painful watching Grandma with her 21-year-old spirit dragging around her 91-year-old body.

So when God took her home on my birthday, I recognized immediately that the entire thing had His wonderful name written all over it. He not only blessed us monetarily, but He relieved me of my duties and my sorrow for Grandma, and gave her a brand new heavenly body.

No, I didn't receive a check in the mail, but God blessed me beyond measure. This is not to say that God will always bless everyone in the same way. Blessings are not always monetary. Those who seek God diligently and trust Him wholeheartedly are blessed with a peace and a sense of purpose that only God can give. All the wealth in the world cannot buy that. God also takes delight in giving us good gifts that He has specifically chosen for us, that have our names written all over them, which tell us, in essence, "I love you and I knew you'd like this."

God's personal gifts

When my grandmother died, she was the last in my immediate family to die. In an eight-year period, I lost my mother, father, brother and grandmother. All the people who were close to me during my childhood and formative years were gone. Our good God knew that in some ways I felt like an orphan. He also knew that that eight-year period had been the toughest in my life.

One morning after Grandma's death, I was listening to my favorite Christian radio station and they spoke a verse that resonated with me, probably because God was speaking to my heart:

Then I will make up to you for the years
That the swarming locust has eaten,
The creeping locust, the stripping locust, and the gnawing locust,
My great army which I sent among you.
And you shall have plenty to eat and be satisfied,
And praise the name of the LORD your God,
Who has dealt wondrously with you;
Then My people will never be put to shame.
JOEL 2:25-26

The locusts had indeed eaten the previous eight years and I knew He was going to bring me to a place of rest and restoration.

My husband and I decided to look for a cabin to purchase as an investment of Grandma's money in our favorite mountain town. We spent an afternoon with a realtor looking at a total of nine cabins and condos. When we walked into the last one—a two-bedroom cabin—I knew I had come "home." It was clear that God had chosen this specifically for us, because it was everything I had ever envisioned in a cabin.

The living room had knotty pine boards on the walls, a wood stove with glass on the front so we could watch the fire, a long covered porch the length of the cabin, and a deck with a hot tub. The cabin was modest and simple, but set up in a small canyon with no other dwellings behind it. The part that really showed me God's hand in it all was the furniture in the cabin. The furniture was surprisingly high quality, and absolutely my taste. We asked the owners if they would consider leaving the furnishings, and we were surprised when they said they would—at no additional cost. The real clincher: I had always wanted a cabin with a buffalo plaid couch—not that I ever expected to get a cabin, much less one with a buffalo plaid couch. Every "girl" has her dream cabin or cottage in her mind. This living room was furnished with a buffalo plaid couch and love seat, and I know they were placed there by the hand of God.

The first weekend we were at the cabin, I had some time alone. My heart was filled to overflowing in gratitude to God, and as I walked through and touched the walls and the furnishings, I thanked Him for his wonderful gifts. The cabin is a healing place for me, and a reminder of God's amazing love.

Give big and He will give bigger

God will always out-give us, if we simply have the faith to first give to Him, and to acknowledge Him in all our ways. God has made it clear through His word that there is a specific order to His formula:

> He who is generous will be blessed
> For he gives some of his food to the poor.
> PROVERBS 22:9

Give first, and then He will give to us. And don't just give, but be generous. Why? Because if we give the five dollars that's in our purse, and hold the ten, God knows that we gave without taking too much of a hit to our pocketbook. And He will give back to us, but without taking much of a hit either, so to speak. But if we give the ten, and hold the five, or maybe even go all out and empty our wallet, He will give back to us in the same way.

> Give, and it will be given to you; good measure, pressed down, shaken together, running over, they will pour into your lap. **For by your standard of measure** it will be measured to you in return.
> LUKE 6:38

Remember the passage from Deuteronomy 24 in the chapter, "Our Heroic God"? It is the same formula:

> When you reap your harvest in the field and have forgotten a sheaf in the field, you shall not go back to get it; it shall be for the alien, for the orphan and for the widow, in order that the LORD your God will bless you in all the work of your hands.
>
> DEUTERONOMY 24:19

And here's another passage of scripture which supports that:

> If there is a poor man with you, one of your brothers, in any of your towns in your land which the LORD your God is giving you, you shall not harden your heart, nor close your hand from your poor brother; but you shall freely open your hand to him, and shall generously lend him sufficient for his need in whatever he lacks. You shall generously give to him, and your heart shall not be grieved when you give to him, because for this thing the LORD your God will bless you in all your work and in all your undertakings.
>
> DEUTERONOMY 15:7-8, 10

Paul also wrote about God's formula:

> Now this I say, he who sows sparingly shall also reap sparingly; and he who sows bountifully shall also reap bountifully.
>
> Let each one do just as he has purposed in his heart; not grudgingly or under compulsion; for God loves a cheerful giver.
>
> And God is able to make all grace abound to you, that always having all sufficiency in everything, **you may have an abundance for every good deed**; as it is written,

"He scattered abroad, he gave to the poor,
His righteousness abides forever."
2 CORINTHIANS 9:6-9

Now you know the formula, see if it works. Test God in this. While it is not wise to test God in other areas, He actually invites you to test Him here. (See the verse from Malachi at the beginning of this chapter.) Give until it hurts a little bit—and do it with a smile, knowing He's going to give back with God-size generosity.

Then wait and see what happens. He delights in surprising you. His reward will come in the least expected way. And you'll know it's from Him, because it's tailored just for you.

Chapter 8

Our God the Destroyer

> There is only one Lawgiver and Judge, the One who
> is able to save and to destroy; but who are you who
> judge your neighbor?
>
> JAMES 4:12

Our God is bent on destroying evil. And He will stop at nothing to do so. Fasten your seatbelt. You are about to see where God's mercy and patience ends, and His judgment begins.

God has two very different sides to Him. As stated above, God saves and God destroys. He is both the compassionate God and the God of justice. For the uninitiated, it should be stated that God goes to extremes in both cases.

Many people close their eyes to God's hard-edged intolerant side, thinking of Him only as a pushover. These are the people who believe that everyone goes to heaven. These are the people who believe that because God is love, He has a very hands-off management style. And these are the people who will someday have a rude awakening.

Thinking of God as one-sided is both ignorant and arrogant. Those who don't want to face God's wrathful side want simply to put Him in a nicely-wrapped box, and keep Him there. And they are living in a dream world.

We must remember that God is wholly and completely righteous. There is no sin or evil in Him. This is His world. He created it, and His desire is first for us to love Him and Him only, and secondly, for righteousness to abound in his creation. God has no patience for evil, or those who perpetuate evil intentionally. They will suffer the consequences.

> "If you are not careful to observe all the words of this law which are written in this book, to fear this honored and awesome name, the LORD your God, then the LORD will bring extraordinary plagues on you and your descendants, even severe and lasting plagues, and miserable and chronic sicknesses.
>
> "And He will bring back on you all the diseases of Egypt of which you were afraid, and they shall cling to you.
>
> "Also every sickness and every plague which, not written in the book of this law, the LORD will bring on you until you are destroyed.
>
> "Then you shall be left few in number, whereas you were as the stars of heaven for multitude, because you did not obey the LORD your God.
>
> "And it shall come about that as the LORD delighted over you to prosper you, and multiply you, so the LORD will delight over you to make you perish and destroy you; and you shall be torn from the land where you are entering to possess it."
>
> DEUTERONOMY 28:58-63

Obey and prosper

This picture of God is not for the faint of heart. And although God, in this case, was speaking to the Israelites before He brought them into the Promised Land, He is the same God today and has the same lack of tolerance for those who don't obey Him.

And what does it mean to obey Him? What are His laws? There are many laws in the Bible—most of them in the Old Testament. (See Exodus, Numbers, Deuteronomy.) He left absolutely no stone unturned when He gave His chosen people His laws. He knew exactly what kinds of sins they could and would commit, and He addressed all of them. Following is an example of His many laws which go on for pages:

> "You shall not see your countryman's ox or his sheep straying away, and pay no attention to them; you shall surely bring them back to your countryman.
>
> "And if your countryman is not near you, or if you do not know him, then you shall bring it home to your house, and it shall remain with you until your countryman looks for it; then you shall restore it to him."
> DEUTERONOMY 22:1-2

And for those who think that God has not thought of everything, consider the following:

> "If two men, a man and his countryman, are struggling together, and the wife of one comes near to deliver her husband from the hand of the one who is striking him, and puts out her hand and seizes his genitals, then you shall cut off her hand; you shall not show pity."
> DEUTERONOMY 25:11-12

Obeying God is not so hard if you have a heart that desires to live graciously and kindly with your fellow man and woman. And if you believe in the blessings that result from following God's laws, you'll gladly do so. But if your heart has evil intent, then God's laws could be stifling.

Then the LORD your God will prosper you abundantly in all the work of your hand, in the offspring of your body and in the offspring of your cattle and in the produce of your ground, for the LORD will again rejoice over you for good, just as He rejoiced over your fathers; if you obey the LORD your God to keep His commandments and His statutes which are written in this book of the law, if you turn to the LORD your God with all your heart and soul.

For this commandment which I command you today **is not too difficult for you**, nor is it out of reach.

It is not in heaven, that you should say, 'Who will go up to heaven for us to get it for us and make us hear it that we may observe it?'

Nor is it beyond the sea, that you should say, 'Who will cross the sea for us to get it for us and make us hear it, that we may observe it?'

But the word is very near you, in your mouth and in your heart, that you may observe it.

DEUTERONOMY 30:9-14

God ensured that His commandments were not too difficult or out of reach for us. Our God the Destroyer, therefore, should only be frightening to those who deliberately choose evil, because He will repay evil with curses, guaranteed.

What wrath? Where?

Why, then, does it seem that so many people are getting away with things without an apparent sign of God's wrath in their lives? There are two reasons. First, God repays in His own time. For example, although Moses was one of the most beloved of God's children, God did not allow him to enter the Promised Land because on one occasion, Moses did not treat God as holy. If God extracted such a price from Moses, you can bet that God has similar expectations for the rest of us. Moses most certainly went to heaven—God personally buried him—but still, he suffered the consequences of not taking God seriously.

Secondly, God tolerates evil only when He knows that good can come out of a situation where evil is present. In this regard, God has amazing self-restraint. He endures watching the people of His world doing hideous things to each other and to its creatures. His God's-eye-view may as well be a horror flick that He watches 24 hours a day, every day. He endures it all because He wants to give everyone opportunities to come to repentance—to confess their sins and proclaim Him Lord of their lives.

However, God's patience has a big caveat: when the ratio of evil to good becomes too great, and there is little or no redeeming value in a person, a city, or even the world as a whole, God has been known to obliterate it. This is because evil is like a virus. It spreads like wildfire. If you don't contain it, it will quickly get out of control.

Too evil, too soon

It wasn't long after the world was created—relatively speaking—that horrific evil had already spread throughout its inhabitants. Genesis Chapter 5 explicitly records the years between when Adam, the first man, was created, and when Noah began building the ark. It was 1,536 years.

> Then the LORD saw that the wickedness of man was great on the earth, and that every intent of the thoughts of his heart **was only evil continually.**
> And the LORD was sorry that He had made man on the earth, and He was grieved in His heart.
> GENESIS 6:5-6

It took only fifteen hundred years for evil to become so rampant that God wanted to wipe out all of creation. To put this into perspective, Adam lived 930 years, so he died about six hundred years before the flood came. Noah was 480 years old when he began building the ark, and 600 when the flood came. Although there were actually ten generations from Adam to Noah, it's important to realize that those ten generations lived an average of 700 to 900 years, so Adam actually lived into Noah's father's generation. Adam watched eight generations of his progeny grow up and have children. And since it only took one more generation before God was ready to obliterate all of the earth's inhabitants, can you imagine the moral decline of mankind that Adam witnessed in his lifetime?

> The Flood was sent because of universal total human depravity, with extreme violence toward others, which warranted severe punishment.[1]

It seems amazing that humanity would take such a short time to go from perfect to universally evil. And it's tragic to think that the beautiful "new" earth would also be wiped out and forever changed with that cataclysmic torrent of water.

> We cannot here reconcile the many complicated geological issues related to the Flood. But, for sure, a cataclysmic, worldwide flood would have had an enormous effect on the surface of the planet. Psalm 104:8 says, "The mountains rose up; the valleys sank down." Oceans deepened due to the weight of water running off land surfaces into them. With the stupendous weight of new runoff water on the earth's mantle, mountains were uplifted. Today, the continents and highest mountains are covered with sea fossils. Half the continental sediments are of oceanic origin. ...Since mountains have waterborne fossils at their highest elevations (including Mt. Everest), it is evident that they were all under water at some time. However, this does not mean the waters had to be deep enough to cover modern Mt. Everest and other high mountains. Mountains were uplifted by the pressures on the earth's mantle.[2]

Sadly, we cannot look around and see what the world looked like when God created it. After the flood, it was markedly different. We couldn't find Eden today even if we wanted to. This is what happens

---

[1]Livingston, Dr. David. "A Universal Flood: 3000 BC." 2005. Ancient Days. 5 January 2010. <http://www.ancientdays.net>

[2]Ibid.

when evil reigns supreme and there is no redeeming value to be found in anyone, except for Noah and his family. It's hard to believe that out of the millions of people on earth before the flood, God saw redeeming qualities in only one family.

> Noah was a righteous man, blameless in his time; Noah walked with God.
>
> GENESIS 6:9B

The last of their kind

To think that Noah was righteous in the midst of so much evil is to know that he was probably saint material. How did it happen that Noah and his family were the last people on earth to worship God? The Bible doesn't tell us, but you could speculate that he was also very lonely in his faith, able only to share it with his wife, children, and their spouses. And when he began building the ark, he took an enormous amount of flak from the people of his community. This is not stated in the Bible, but you can easily assume that if there was that much evil, there was that much back-biting.

That's not surprising, considering he was building a boat with an interior space equaling over 800 railroad box cars,[3] and it took him 120 years to do so. The ark would be nearly the size of the Titanic. No one had ever seen a boat of that magnitude.

The 120 years required to build the ark was actually a grace period given by God to the people of the world. During that time, not only was Noah chief builder, cook and bottle washer, he also served the role of preacher. 1 Peter 3:18-20 infers that Christ in the Spirit preached through Noah to the antediluvians (the people who existed before the flood). God gave those people ample time to clean up their act and come to repentance—about one and a half the length of an average lifetime nowadays. On the "Patient God" vs. "Not-So-Patient

---

[3]MacDonald, William. "Genesis." Believer's Bible Commentary. Nashville, TN: Thomas Nelson Publishers, 1995.

God" scoreboard, this was definitely a mark for the patient side. This was like having to put up with an obnoxious, angry, ungrateful, in-your-face relative in your house for 120 years.

It clearly required God's unearthly patience to watch evil grow like gangrene while His beloved Noah and his family took years of verbal and possibly physical abuse. The sad thing is, even with all of Noah's preaching, no one came to repentance. God was right. These people were evil through and through, but God didn't want them to have any excuse when they came before Him at judgment.

Eight people emerged from the ark when the flood subsided: Noah and his wife; his three sons, Shem, Ham and Japheth; and their three wives. It was up to Shem, Ham and Japheth (and their wives) to repopulate the earth, and to teach their children and their children's children to follow God's laws, so that future generations could avoid the evil ways of the antideluvians.

Evil had grown up again

Unfortunately, it was only about 400 years and nine generations later (when counting the generations since Shem) that some of the people on earth had become so evil that God decided to destroy two cities: Sodom and Gomorrah.

We enter the story when Abraham was entertaining three unexpected visitors. The visitors had actually come to tell him that Isaac, the son God promised he would conceive with Sarah, would be born in a year. Abraham eventually realized they were heavenly visitors: two were angels and the third was a preincarnate appearance of Jesus. The Lord told Abraham that He was going to destroy the two cities.

> And the LORD said, "The outcry of Sodom and Gomorrah is indeed great, and their sin is exceedingly grave.
>
> "I will go down now, and see if they have done entirely according to its outcry, which has come to Me; and if not, I will know."
>
> Then the men turned away from there and went toward Sodom, while Abraham was still standing before the LORD.

And Abraham came near and said, "Wilt Thou indeed sweep away the righteous with the wicked?

"Suppose there are fifty righteous within the city; wilt Thou indeed sweep it away and not spare the place for the sake of the fifty righteous who are in it?

"Far be it from Thee to do such a thing, to slay the righteous with the wicked, so that the righteous and the wicked are treated alike. Far be it from Thee! Shall not the Judge of all the earth deal justly?"

So the LORD said, "If I find in Sodom fifty righteous within the city, then I will spare the whole place on their account."

And Abraham answered and said, "Now behold, I have ventured to speak to the LORD, although I am but dust and ashes.

"Suppose the fifty righteous are lacking five, wilt Thou destroy the whole city because of five?" And He said, "I will not destroy it if I find forty-five there."

And he spoke to Him yet again and said, "Suppose forty are found there?" And He said, "I will not do it on account of the forty."

Then he said, "Oh may the LORD not be angry, and I shall speak; suppose thirty are found there?" And He said, "I will not do it if I find thirty there."

And he said, "Now behold, I have ventured to speak to the LORD; suppose twenty are found there?" And He said, "I will not destroy it on account of the twenty."

Then he said, "Oh may the LORD not be angry, and I shall speak only this once; suppose ten are found there?" And He said, "I will not destroy it on account of the ten."

And as soon as He had finished speaking to Abraham the LORD departed; and Abraham returned to his place.

GENESIS 18:20-33

When the Lord told Abraham what He was about to do, Abraham's reaction was typical: "What? You mean you aren't the loving, benevolent God we all expect you to be?" The answer is that God is patient with those He knows will come to repentance. For those who will simply continue in their corrupt ways and whose lives do nothing but produce evil, there is no point in prolonging them.

Blatant and unrelenting evil

After listening patiently to Abraham, the Lord did go to Sodom. The angels, who had gone ahead, were staying at the house of Lot, Abraham's nephew. The men of Sodom were so evil that when they found out that two new "men" had entered town, they wanted to have sexual relations with them. The men of Sodom stormed Lot's house and demanded that they bring out the two "men." Lot was so desperate to protect the angels that he offered his two daughters to the men of the town. Whether Lot knew his guests were angels or not is unclear, but he knew they were holy men of some kind, and felt obligated to protect his guests over his daughters—a choice no father should have to make. But Sodom's men didn't want his daughters. And when they went to break down the door, the angels struck all of the town's men with blindness so that they couldn't even find the door.

The members of Lot's immediate family were the only righteous people the angels found in Sodom. Lot's daughters were both engaged, and even his prospective sons-in-law laughed when he told them they needed to leave. So when the morning dawned and the two cities were scheduled for immediate destruction, only Lot, his wife and daughters were urged to leave Sodom—less than ten people, just as the Lord had predicted. There is no record of any righteous people found in Gomorrah.

The Lord did as He said, and waited until Lot and his family had exited the city. However, the angels had instructed Lot and his family not to look back. Their directive was both literal and figurative. While Lot and his family were considered righteous enough to be saved, Lot had chosen to live in Sodom and no doubt had been influenced by—and may even have liked—the Sodom lifestyle. Sodomy was not Sodom's only evil. Ezekiel 16:49 also lists arrogance, abundant food, careless ease and a lack of helping the poor and needy as its other sins. So when the angels told Lot and his family not to look back, they meant that they needed to turn away from that lifestyle entirely.

Apparently Lot's wife needed one last look, and when she did, she was turned into a pillar of salt. This is an example of what happens when people do not take God's messengers seriously. The fire and brimstone that rained down from heaven was so hot that when Abraham looked toward Sodom and Gomorrah, "the smoke of the land ascended like the smoke of a furnace." (Genesis 19:28) According to the *Matthew Henry Complete Commentary on the Whole Bible*:

> It was an utter ruin, and irreparable. That fruitful valley remains to this day a great lake, or dead sea; it is called the Salt Sea, Num. 34:12. Travellers [sic] say that it is about thirty miles long and ten miles broad; it has no living creature in it; it is not moved by the wind; the smell of it is offensive; things do not easily sink in it. The Greeks call it Asphaltites, from a sort of pitch which it casts up. Jordan falls into it, and is lost there.[4]

God has no patience for blatant evil. And He ensured that that area of the world would remain as a reminder of what happens to those who practice such evil, and have no intention of pursuing righteousness.

Have no pity

Deuteronomy has many references to God's judgment on certain matters, most notably Israel's stubborn affinity for idol worship.

> "If your brother, your mother's son, or your son or daughter, or the wife you cherish, or your friend who is as your own soul, entice you secretly, saying, 'Let us go and serve other gods' (whom neither you nor your

---

[4] Henry, Matthew. "Genesis 19." Matthew Henry Commentary on the Whole Bible (Complete). 2010. Crosswalk.com. 6 January 2010. <http://www.crosswalk.com>

fathers have known, of the gods of the peoples who are around you, near you or far from you, from one end of the earth to the other end), you shall not yield to him or listen to him, and your eye shall not pity him, nor shall you spare or conceal him.

"But you shall surely kill him; your hand shall be first against him to put him to death, and afterwards the hand of all the people.

"So you shall stone him to death because he has sought to seduce you from the LORD your God who brought you out from the land of Egypt, out of the house of slavery.

"Then all Israel will hear and be afraid, and will never again do such a wicked thing among you."

DEUTERONOMY 13:6-11

God underlines it again in another chapter of Deuteronomy:

"If there is found in your midst, in any of your towns, which the LORD your God is giving you, a man or a woman who does what is evil in the sight of the LORD your God, by transgressing His covenant, and has gone and served other gods and worshiped them, or the sun or the moon or any of the heavenly host, which I have not commanded, and if it is told you and you have heard of it, then you shall inquire thoroughly. And behold, if it is true and the thing certain that this detestable thing has been done in Israel, then you shall bring out that man or that woman who has done this evil deed, to your gates, that is, the man or the woman, and you shall stone them to death."

DEUTERONOMY 17:2-5

When God gave the Israelites these instructions, He was preparing them to enter the Promised Land. They had been wandering in the wilderness for 40 years, and they had had no outside influence. Now they would have to go into the Promised Land, and with God's help, defeat the peoples of seven different nations who were living there. God knew that if they intermingled with the natives who were idol worshippers, the Israelites would surely be turned away from Him, just as someone who is given a thousand dollars and placed on Rodeo Drive will almost as surely walk away with loaded shopping bags.

God had called the nation of Israel to Himself, and He had to make the rules clear and the stakes high before He turned them loose in sin city. If they transgressed into idol worshipping, there would be no mercy and no second chances. God had plans for this people. The lineage of His Son Jesus would come through this people. This was the only nation that, after the Great Flood, acknowledged and worshipped Him as the only true God. He had to keep the Israelites pure, or He would have another antediluvian world on His hands. This was another example of God going about destroying sin before it spread like a virus.

> "Then the LORD your God shall bring you into the land where you are entering to possess it, and shall clear away many nations before you, the Hittites and the Girgashites and the Amorites and the Canaanites and the Perizzites and Hivites and the Jebusites, seven nations greater and stronger than you, and when the LORD your God shall deliver them before you, and you shall defeat them, then you shall utterly destroy them. You shall make no covenant with them and show no favor to them.
>
> "Furthermore, you shall not intermarry with them; you shall not give your daughters to their sons, nor shall you take their daughters for your sons.
>
> "For they will turn your sons away from following Me to serve other gods; then the anger of the LORD will be kindled against you, and He will quickly destroy you.

"But thus you shall do to them: you shall tear down their altars, and smash their sacred pillars, and hew down their Asherim, [the female goddess counterpart of Baal] and burn their graven images with fire.

"For you are a holy people to the LORD your God; the LORD your God has chosen you to be a people for His own possession out of all the peoples who are on the face of the earth.

"The LORD did not set His love on you nor choose you because you were more in number than any of the peoples, for you were the fewest of all peoples, but because the LORD loved you and kept the oath which He swore to your forefathers, the LORD brought you out by a mighty hand, and redeemed you from the house of slavery, from the hand of Pharaoh, king of Egypt.

"Know therefore that the LORD your God, He is God, the faithful God, who keeps His covenant and His lovingkindness to a thousandth generation with those who love Him and keep His commandments; but repays those who hate Him to their faces, to destroy them; He will not delay with him who hates Him, He will repay him to his face."

DEUTERONOMY 7:1-10

When God demonstrates no patience and swift retribution in regard to certain sins, it's because He alone knows the long-term ramifications. He sees the future devastation when evil is left unchecked. We have to trust that His intent is for our greater good.

Had He left the world the way it was before the Great Flood, we would either have caused our own extinction long ago, or we would be living in a world rife with hate and terror. Had God not instructed the Israelites to keep to themselves when they entered Canaan, and to destroy the peoples who worshipped other gods, the Israelites would have eventually taken on the belief system of those nations. And then the world would be awash with various forms of idolatry and evil, and God would have been reduced in their minds to just another god.

And when Gabriel came to Mary to tell her she would be the mother of the Messiah, Mary might have said, "Who?" instead of proclaiming that marvelous and beautiful Magnificat (Luke 1:46-55). And Jesus would have had no remnant people who remembered God's promises of a Messiah or the prophecies surrounding Him. And had no one remembered God or His promises, Jesus would have had to start at square one. Just as God did after the Great Flood.

So, you see, it's imperative that God plays hardball at times. He has to take a stand against wickedness and deal with it swiftly and surely. He has to preserve the holiness of His beloved people lest they get swept away in the tides of temptation and the subtleties of a God-less society.

Chapter 9

Our Testing God

"If a prophet or a dreamer of dreams arises among you and gives you a sign or a wonder, and the sign or the wonder comes true, concerning which he spoke to you, saying, 'Let us go after other gods (whom you have not known) and let us serve them,' you shall not listen to the words of that prophet or that dreamer of dreams; for the LORD your God is testing you to find out if you love the LORD your God with all your heart and with all your soul."

DEUTERONOMY 13:1-3

For those who work in the retail industry, the testing side of God is like having a secret shopper in your midst. You know that at any time, a secret shopper—paid by your boss—is testing you to see how you perform. You don't know who it is, so you'd better be on your toes at all times. And you can pretty much bet that the secret shopper will appear on one of those days when everything is going wrong and your attitude is anything but stellar.

God tests His children for a variety of reasons. One of the reasons, as explained in the verses above, is to see if we love Him, and will follow Him only. At first glance, this kind of test looks fairly easy to pass. In fact, in the next verse, God even tells you how to pass it:

> "You shall follow the LORD your God and fear Him;
> and you shall keep His commandments, listen to His
> voice, serve Him, and cling to Him."
> DEUTERONOMY 13:4

But before you consider this test a no-brainer, consider the story of a man of God, whose name is not mentioned in the Bible, but who failed a similar test and lost his life because of it.

This "man of God" was instructed by God to warn Jeroboam, the king of Israel, about the calamity that would soon befall him because of his idolatry. Jeroboam had built two different houses of worship in high places, and each had a golden calf and an altar. If that wasn't enough to spark the Lord God to anger, Jeroboam appointed priests that were not of the tribe of Levi—the only tribe from which priests could be appointed, according to God's commandment stated in Numbers 3:5-10. Jeroboam also appointed a religious feast day which was not ordained by God.

Because Jeroboam had departed so far from God's laws, the man of God came to him as he was burning incense at the idolatrous altar at Bethel. Curiously, the man of God did not denounce Jeroboam, but instead directed his prophecy toward the altar itself:

> And he cried against the altar by the word of the LORD,
> and said, "O altar, altar, thus says the LORD, 'Behold,
> a son shall be born to the house of David, Josiah by
> name; and on you he shall sacrifice the priests of the
> high places who burn incense on you, and human
> bones shall be burned on you.'"
> 1 KINGS 13:2

Don't read past this until you get a mental picture of what the man of God prophesied. *Humans would eventually be burned on that very altar.*

> Then he gave a sign the same day, saying, "This is the
> sign which the LORD has spoken, 'Behold the altar shall
> be split apart and the ashes which are on it shall be
> poured out.'"
>
> 1 KINGS 13:3

Jeroboam was not one to stand for such insubordination, and he stretched out his hand toward the prophet, and screamed at his guards, "Seize him!" To his utter shock, his hand shriveled up, the altar split in two, and the ashes were poured out.

Staring at his hand, which "he could not draw back to himself," Jeroboam had a sudden epiphany. *"Please entreat the LORD your God, and pray for me, that my hand may be restored to me,"* he said. The man of God did so, and Jeroboam's hand was restored.

> Then the king said to the man of God, "Come home with
> me and refresh yourself, and I will give you a reward."
>
> But the man of God said to the king, "If you were
> to give me half your house I would not go with you,
> nor would I eat bread or drink water in this place.
>
> "For so it was commanded me by the word of the
> LORD, saying, 'You shall eat no bread, nor drink water,
> nor return by the way which you came.'"
>
> So he went another way, and did not return by the
> way which he came to Bethel.
>
> 1 KINGS 13:7-10

God was apparently trying to keep temptation away from His spokesperson. *The Believer's Bible Commentary* has this to say:

> If the king could not silence the prophet by threats, he
> would try by gaining his fellowship. God had issued
> strict instructions to the prophet that he was to do
> nothing to indicate the slightest tolerance of Jeroboam's
> evil reign.[1]

---

[1]MacDonald, William. "1 Kings." Farstad, Art, ed. Believer's Bible Commentary. Nashville, TN: Thomas Nelson Publishers, 1995.

Unexpected and unlikely temptation

So far, the man of God was staying between the lines. However, there was a test waiting for him—not necessarily ordained by God, but not prevented, either. The news of what had happened to Jeroboam spread quickly, and an old prophet living in Bethel heard about it from his sons. He wanted to meet the man of God, and asked them which way he had gone. The old prophet's sons told him, and he saddled up his donkey and went after him. He found the man of God sitting under an oak tree.

> Then he [the old prophet] said to him, "Come home with me and eat bread."
>
> And he said, "I cannot return with you, nor go with you, nor will I eat bread or drink water with you in this place. For a command came to me by the word of the LORD, 'You shall eat no bread, nor drink water there; do not return by going the way which you came.'"
>
> And he said to him, "I also am a prophet like you, and an angel spoke to me by the word of the LORD, saying, 'Bring him back with you to your house, that he may eat bread and drink water.'" But he lied to him.
>
> 1 KINGS 13:15-18

Why did the old prophet lie to him? Maybe the man of God had gained some renown for what had happened in the high place with Jeroboam, and the old prophet wanted to have the local celebrity at his house. Two commentaries suggest that the old "prophet"—who may not have been God's prophet at all, but rather someone who wanted to gain favor with Jeroboam—wanted to throw temptation into the man of God's path, and expose him as a fake. It's hard to say, but his lie cost the man of God his life, because he believed him and went home with him.

> Now it came about, as they were sitting down at the table, that the word of the LORD came to the prophet who had brought him back; and he cried to the man of God who

came from Judah, saying, "Thus says the LORD, 'Because you have disobeyed the command of the LORD, and have not observed the commandment which the LORD your God commanded you, but have returned and eaten bread and drunk water in the place of which He said to you, "Eat no bread and drink no water"; your body shall not come to the grave of your fathers.'"

And it came about after he had eaten bread and after he had drunk, that he saddled the donkey for him, for the prophet whom he had brought back.

Now when he had gone, a lion met him on the way and killed him, and his body was thrown on the road, with the donkey standing beside it; the lion also was standing beside the body.

1 KINGS 13:20-24

While it doesn't seem plausible that the "old prophet" was truly a man of God, nonetheless, God can speak through anyone, and when He speaks, the person through whom He speaks can do nothing but give utterance.

A higher call, stricter standards

The man of God paid a high price for not heeding God's commands, while the old prophet got away without any apparent repercussions. It smacks of injustice. But God has higher expectations of His prophets because they are His mouthpiece. Because the old prophet did not receive the kind of punishment that the "man of God" did, it's almost a dead giveaway (no pun intended) that the "old prophet" was a fake.

We know that the man of God's death by the attack of a lion was ordained by God, because the lion did not tear up his body, nor did it attack the donkey, or any of the passersby. Instead it stood there until enough people had witnessed and documented its unusual behavior. The fact that the donkey did not flee from the lion is also a mark of God's presence.

Although the man of God's death seems tragic, we can't assume that he suffered. While God wanted to discipline him, and to make him an example for future prophets who carried the weighty responsibility of speaking for God, still God loved him, and undoubtedly took him to heaven.

God jealously guards His holy reputation, and that is one aspect of His character that is nonnegotiable. Had the man of God disregarded God's instructions and gotten away with it, God's credibility would be damaged. God is consistent and He follows through; on that we can depend. Just as a parent who sets boundaries and must follow through when they are breached, even when it breaks the parent's heart to inflict the punishment, still it must be done for the greater good of the errant child, and to set an example for the siblings.

God also tests those He has huge plans for—like Abraham. Abraham was a true man of God and God clearly loved him, because He made a covenant with him which would be the foundation of the Hebrew nation, and ultimately, the Christian church. And perhaps that's why He tested him—because Abraham would be the patriarch of the Israelites, and later, all Christianity. Abraham would have to demonstrate the kind of God-walk that was worthy of the responsibility with which he would be endowed.

In the covenant with Abraham, God promised that although he and his wife were way past child-bearing age, a son would be born to them, and from this son—Isaac—their descendants would be as numerous as the stars. Those descendants would be the Israelite nation, the chosen people—today's Jews—and God would ultimately bring them into Canaan, the promised land. More than that, Jesus, the Savior of the world, would come through Abraham's lineage, and He would be the Savior of not only the Jews but the Gentiles as well. So Abraham would literally be the father of the Jewish faith and the Christian church!

God, therefore, had high expectations of Abraham. So God put Abraham to the ultimate test. When his son Isaac was 17, God instructed Abraham to do a strange and painful task:

> And He said, "Take now your son, your only son, whom you love, Isaac, and go to the land of Moriah; and offer him there as a burnt offering on one of the mountains of which I will tell you."
>
> GENESIS 22:2

Clearly, God knew how dearly beloved Isaac was to Abraham, and it isn't hard to imagine what must have been going through Abraham's mind at such a request. Yet the Bible records no spoken objections from Abraham, but rather complete obedience and quiet faith. He remembered God's promise to him that Isaac would be the one through whom the covenant would be fulfilled:

> But God said, "No, but Sarah your wife shall bear you a son, and you shall call his name Isaac; and I will establish My covenant with him for an everlasting covenant for his descendants after him."
>
> "But My covenant I will establish with Isaac, whom Sarah will bear to you at this season next year."
>
> GENESIS 17:19, 21

As they prepared for the three-day journey to Mount Moriah, Abraham strapped the wood for the burnt offering on the back of his son, Isaac, while he carried the implements to make the fire, and the knife. Abraham did not tell Isaac that he was the intended sacrifice, because Abraham expected God to intercede. This is evidenced by the heart-wrenching scene between Abraham and his only son, as Isaac inquired in his innocence:

> "Behold, the fire and the wood, but where is the lamb for the burnt offering?"
>
> And Abraham said, "God will provide for Himself the lamb for the burnt offering, my son." And the two of them walked on together.
>
> GENESIS 22:7B-8

When they reached the place which God designated for him to build an altar and still there was no message from God, Abraham constructed the altar. Abraham must have taken his sweet time, but eventually, the altar was completed and all was ready. Still, God did not make His presence known, so Abraham bound Isaac and laid him on the altar on top of the wood. Isaac must have allowed him to do so, because Abraham was then 117 years old to Isaac's 17, and Isaac could have had the upper hand if he'd put his mind to it.

Where are You, God?

Scripture tells us that Abraham began to believe that perhaps God would not intercede, but would, instead, let Isaac be sacrificed and then raise him from the dead—because God had said Isaac would be the one through whom his descendants would come.

> By faith Abraham, when he was tested, offered up Isaac; and he who had received the promises was offering up his only begotten son; it was he to whom it was said, "In Isaac your descendants shall be called." He considered that God is able to raise men even from the dead, from which he also received him back as a type.
> HEBREWS 11:17-19

There had been no record of God raising anyone from the dead from the beginning of the world until Abraham's time, but Abraham's faith in God and His promises was so complete that he made up such a possibility in his mind, and it gave him enough comfort to follow through with God's directions. Yet that did not obscure the horrible prospect of having to stab his son to keep him from burning alive.

Still, he was obedient and it was only when he raised the knife to slay his son that he heard from heaven.

> But the angel of the LORD called to him from heaven, and said, "Abraham, Abraham!" And he said, "Here I am."

> And he said, "Do not stretch out your hand against the lad, and do nothing to him; for now I know that you fear God, since you have not withheld your son, your only son, from Me."
>
> Then Abraham raised his eyes and looked, and behold, behind him a ram caught in the thicket by his horns; and Abraham went and took the ram, and offered him up for a burnt offering in the place of his son.
>
> GENESIS 22:11-13

Although Abraham passed this test with flying colors, there were other tests at which he failed miserably. It's comforting to know that he was just as human as the rest of us. If you feel that God is testing you in a certain area of your life, you can rejoice, because it means He plans to use you in a powerful way.

Like a sword in His hands

God wants to turn us into strong, shining weapons for the faith, and to do so, He has to put us through an extensive process which at times seems like punishment. But consider how Samurai swords— known for their keen sharpness of the blade—are made.

> To make a blade like those used in the Katana [the Samurai swords], the Japanese swordsmiths had to overcome a problem that had baffled all armourers for years. Swordmakers could make steel very hard so that it would hold a sharp edge, but by doing this they made the blade very brittle. However, soft steel would not break so easily but would not hold a sharp edge and would quickly dull in battle. Most swordmakers would go for something in between, so it was reasonably sharp and sturdy.
>
> One way the Japanese swordsmiths solved the problem was to hammer together layers of steel varying in hardness, welding them into a metal sandwich. This was then reheated and hammered out thin again. This process was carried out **dozens of times** until

the steel contained thousands of paper-thin lamina-
tions of hard and soft metal. It was then hammered
into the right shape and was ready for the final step.
This is where the swordsmith would cover the top
half of the blade with a layer of adhesive material,
which usually consisted of clay. The blade was then
heated to a temperature that made the blade glow
to the smith's liking, and then a prayer was said and
the blade was plunged into water. The exposed edge
cooled instantly while the rest of the blade, protected
by the clay, cooled slowly and remained comparatively
soft. The final result was a sword blade of a soft non-
brittle metal that shows on the bottom a thin line that
was to be sharpened to become the actual blade. This
produced an extremely sharp and robust sword.

This was not a speedy process and did not come
cheap as it took many days to make and several people
to help with the process of heating the blade, but the
end product was, and still is, regarded as a priceless
item. To make an inscription on the sword was not
uncommon. The swordsmith usually put on his name,
his titles and where it was made.[2]

Remember the Israelites who moaned and complained in the
wilderness, and went against God's commandments against idols
only days after hearing them from His very mouth? Our Swordsmith
wanted to make them into strong, sharp weapons who would be able
to enter the Promised Land and conquer nation upon nation in the
name of the Only True God. He wanted to put His name and title on
His beloved Israelite "swords," so He honed and tested them for years
in the wilderness. They would be the people who would represent
Him through generations to come.

---

[2]"The Samurai Sword." 6 July 2000. BBC Homepage h2g2. 8 January 2010
< www.bbc.co.uk/dna/h2h2/A364213>

> "Now then, if you will indeed obey My voice and keep
> My covenant, then you shall be My own possession
> among all the peoples, for all the earth is Mine; and you
> shall be to Me a kingdom of priests and a holy nation."
> EXODUS 19:5-6A

From them would come the first priests on earth, and to them He would entrust His written Word. This holy nation would observe, preserve and record the Word of God. He knew that when they came through the heating and hammering, their worth to the world would be priceless. The Israelites' responsibility over the Word of God was huge, because it is not merely words on paper. The Word of God is living—it literally has power—and is *even sharper* than a Samurai sword.

> For the word of God is **living and active and sharper
> than any two-edged sword**, and piercing as far as the
> division of soul and spirit, of both joints and marrow, and
> able to judge the thoughts and intentions of the heart.
> HEBREWS 4:12

Would God have anyone wielding a weapon with such power—His Word—if they were anything less than capable? Would you send a child to do the work of a warrior? No—you must first be proven, tested, sharpened.

So if you feel that you are being put through the fire, know that God has grand plans and high expectations for you. God wants to make you holy, and to wield you like a flashing sword in His mighty hand.

Chapter 10

Our God of Wonders

And Isaiah said, "This shall be the sign to you from the LORD, that the LORD will do the thing that He has spoken: shall the shadow go forward ten steps or go back ten steps?"

So Hezekiah answered, "It is easy for the shadow to decline ten steps; no, but let the shadow turn backward ten steps."

And Isaiah the prophet cried to the LORD, and He brought the shadow on the stairway back ten steps by which it had gone down to the stairway of Ahaz.

2 KINGS 20:9-11

A shadow going backward ten steps. A hand—just a hand—writing on a wall. The sun staying put in the sky for an extra day. A donkey talking. Fire and brimstone raining from heaven. A storm's fury calmed by a few words. If anyone ever tells you that the Bible is boring—or if you have ever said such a thing yourself—you have not really read God's marvelous Word, and encountered the God of wonders.

There is nothing that God cannot—and will not—do for His beloved children. And He doesn't do them to entertain us as a magician would. He commands the natural to become supernatural to keep us from the clutches of the enemy, to give us a small glimpse of His magnificent glory, to answer a fervent prayer, or to give us a wake-up call when we have run short on faith.

Or, He might do something absolutely show-stopping simply to usher his chosen people into the Promised Land, and to say, in essence, "Welcome home."

When Joshua was to lead the sons of Israel into Canaan after they had traveled for forty years in the wilderness, they first had to cross the Jordan River. The Jordan is not a big river, nor particularly wide, nor especially tumultuous. The Israelites would have been able to cross it without any supernatural help. But this was a special day: the Israelites were finally going to claim their inheritance, and the covenant that God had made with Abraham was at last being fulfilled. So God made the river stop at the city of Adam upstream, and enabled the Israelites to cross on dry ground.

What's key about this is that the water upstream did not stop flowing. It continued at the same pace, but suddenly began to gather in a heap.

> So it came about when the people set out from their tents to cross the Jordan with the priests carrying the ark of the covenant before the people, and when those who carried the ark came into the Jordan, and the feet of the priests carrying the ark were dipped in the edge of the water (for the Jordan overflows all its banks all the days of harvest), that the waters which were flowing down from above stood and rose up in one heap, a great distance away at Adam, the city that is beside Zarethan; and those which were flowing down toward the sea of the Arabah, the Salt Sea, were completely cut off. So the people crossed opposite Jericho.
> JOSHUA 3:14-16

God had parted the Red Sea forty years before as he ushered His chosen people out of Egypt and away from the pursuing Egyptians. God made sure that they were ushered into the Promised Land with a similar flourish, so that they would know that He, the Lord their God who had brought them out of Egypt, was bringing them into Canaan just as He, Yahweh, "the keeper of the covenant," said He would.

There was also another reason for this dramatic entrance into Canaan: God had a specific time schedule in mind. The Israelites crossed the Jordan exactly five days short of a full forty years since the exodus from Egypt, and five days before Passover. God wanted them safely in their new land so they could celebrate Passover, for they had come full circle: the angel of death who had killed all the first-born of the Egyptians "passed over" the houses of the Israelites who sprinkled the blood of the lamb on their doorposts just before they left Egypt, and now they would celebrate their arrival into their land with their annual Passover celebration. God's timing is always perfect.

How God stopped the waters of the Jordan "in a heap" can only be imagined. Some commentaries suggest that a landslide blocked the river, but God needs no landslide to make water pile up in a heap, just as there were no apparent dams to push the Red Sea back on both sides. And had a landslide blocked the river, that landslide would have had to be removed miraculously, because as soon as all of the Israelites had crossed, the waters returned to their place. Interestingly, the verse in Joshua about the Jordan standing "in a heap" is cross-referenced with Exodus 15:8 (referring to the parting of the Red Sea):

> And at the blast of Thy nostrils the waters were piled up,
> The flowing waters **stood up like a heap;**
> The deeps were congealed in the heart of the sea.

The Hebrew word for "stood up" in Exodus is *nâtsab*, which means "to be set up, to be stationed, to station oneself, to stand, to be firm or healthy, to set, to place, to erect." The waters of the Red Sea weren't just pushed back, they stood at attention before the Lord God Almighty. You can bet that the waters of the Jordan stood erect in just the same manner before the kingship of He who made them.

> For the LORD your God dried up the waters of the Jordan before you until you had crossed, just as the LORD your God had done to the Red Sea, which he dried up before us until we had crossed; that all the peoples of the earth may know that the hand of the LORD is mighty, so that you may fear the LORD your God forever.
>
> JOSHUA 4:23-24

God stopped the water about fifteen miles upstream because hundreds of thousands of people, their livestock, tents and belongings had to get across. The crossing took anywhere from several hours to nearly a day. The wall of Jordan water, climbing ever higher, must have been something to see.

Joshua, who had been Moses' understudy all the years they wandered through the wilderness, witnessed first-hand all the wonders that God wrought for the Israelites. He and another man named Caleb were the only two men who survived from the original Israelite nation that came from Egypt and made it to the Promised Land. Because of the Israelites' disobedience and grumbling, God ensured that the entire generation of Israelites who had come from Egypt died in the wilderness. Only the new generation who had been born during the forty years of wilderness travel would cross the Jordan, except for Joshua and Caleb. Even Moses had failed to treat the Lord as holy in one instance, and was barred from crossing the Jordan and died just after the Lord allowed him to see the land from atop a nearby mountain.

It was a good thing that Joshua had seen the mighty works of God, because he was going to need a good dose of faith when he saw what he was up against in the Promised Land. God had told them they would possess the land, but that didn't mean possession would come free. Canaan—the land of milk and honey—was inhabited by many different peoples, all of whom were morally perverse. The Israelites, with God's help, would have to clean house. So Joshua began doing just that, beginning with Jericho.

When the people of Jericho heard about the arrival of the sons of Israel, they shut the city up tight. No one went out and no one came in. Israel's reputation had preceded them. Rahab, a harlot who hid two of Joshua's spies, told them why all of Jericho feared the sons of Israel:

> Now before they lay down [where she was hiding them on the roof] she came up to them on the roof, and said to the men, "I know that the LORD has given you the land, and that the terror of you has fallen on us, and that all the inhabitants of the land have melted away before you.
>
> "For we have heard how the LORD dried up the water of the Red Sea before you when you came out of Egypt, and what you did to the two kings of the Amorites who were beyond the Jordan, to Sihon and Og, whom you utterly destroyed.
>
> "And when we heard it, our hearts melted and no courage remained in any man any longer because of you; for the LORD your God, He is God in heaven above and on earth beneath.
>
> JOSHUA 2:8-11

Jericho was fortified by high walls and gates. Its citizens knew all too well that they weren't just trying to hold out the Israelites but God Himself. They might as well have been beavers trying to dam the Mississippi River. The *Key Word Study Bible's* explanatory notes say:

> This was not a mere military confrontation with a people who were entrenched in a formidable stronghold. The implications are more spiritual than political. God was bringing judgment upon those who had long refused Him and was working on behalf of that people with whom He had just renewed His covenant. The fall of Jericho cogently taught the Canaanites that

Israel's successes were not mere human victories of man against man but victories of the God of Israel over their gods.[1]

God told Joshua and the Israelites to march around the city once a day for six days, and on the seventh day they were to march around seven times, blowing their trumpets. Their marching did nothing to the wall, but probably kept the inhabitants of Jericho on edge for a week. Their trumpets served only to herald the mighty arm of God, because this was God's battle. For just as the sons of Israel completed that seventh trip around the wall, the walls fell down. And they didn't fall down as most walls fall down, with rubble everywhere—they fell down *flat*. Flatter than a pancake. *Flat*. As though there was never a wall there. One commentary describes it as possibly being like an elevator going down into the ground. When God does miracles, He makes sure there is no mistake that His hand was in it.

> So the people shouted, and priests blew the trumpets; and it came about, when the people heard the sound of the trumpet, that the people shouted with a great shout and the wall fell down flat, so that the people went up into the city, **every man straight ahead,** and they took the city.
>
> JOSHUA 6:20

No man had to move sideways to avoid a boulder or a jagged piece of masonry. One moment, a high wall stood before them, and the next moment, they were staring at the exposed city. Perhaps, like the scene in Numbers (16:31-32), the ground simply opened up and swallowed up the walls. Even the Israelites who had become accustomed to witnessing miracles must have paused a moment in shock before rushing into the city.

---

[1]"Joshua." Spiros Zodhiates, Th.D., ex. ed. <u>Hebrew-Greek Key Word Study Bible</u>. Chattanooga, TN: AMG Publishers, 1990.

God had told Joshua when He commissioned him to be the leader of the Israelites that He would always be with him. Always. What a comfort. When God is with you, there is NOTHING you can't do.

> "No man will be able to stand before you all the days of your life. Just as I have been with Moses, **I will be with you; I will not fail you or forsake you.**
>
> "Be strong and courageous, for you shall give this people possession of the land which I swore to their fathers to give them.
>
> "Only be strong and very courageous, be careful to do according to all the law which Moses My servant commanded you; do not turn from it to the right or to the left, so that you may have success wherever you go.
>
> "This book of the law shall not depart from your mouth, but you shall meditate on it day and night, so that you may be careful to do according to all that is written in it, for then you will make your way prosperous, and then you will have success.
>
> "Have I not commanded you? Be strong and courageous! Do not tremble or be dismayed, **for the LORD your God is with you wherever you go.**"
>
> JOSHUA 1:5-9

Joshua didn't have to be afraid, because he knew his Commander would always be with him. God would give him what he needed to possess the land. Nonetheless, Joshua had to be courageous, because God was sending him into battles where the odds almost always looked bleak.

With the conquest of Jericho under their belts, it wasn't long before Israel gained a reputation as mighty warriors who were intent on conquering the land. After Jericho, the Israelites captured the city of Ai, and therefore the great city of Gibeon decided to ally itself with Israel so that it would be spared. However, the five Amorite kings of Jerusalem, Hebron, Jarmuth, Lachish and Eglon weren't about to surrender without a fight, and were particularly annoyed with Gibeon for allying itself with the foreigners. So they attacked Gibeon, and Gibeon sent word to Joshua, asking the Israelites to come to their aid.

God told Joshua that he would win the battle. So Joshua and the Israelites marched uphill, all night, more than twenty-five miles until they arrived at Gibeon. The warriors were exhausted but God made up for their waning energy, because it was *He* who fought the battle for them—literally.

> And the LORD confounded them before Israel, and He slew them with a great slaughter at Gibeon, and pursued them by the way of the ascent of Beth-horon, and struck them as far as Azekah and Makkedah.
>
> And it came about as they fled from before Israel, while they were at the descent of Beth-horon, that the LORD threw large stones from heaven on them as far as Azekah, and they died; there were more who died from the hailstones than those whom the sons of Israel killed with the sword.
>
> JOSHUA 10:10-11

The Israelites surprised the enemy, but that would not have been enough to give them an edge. The Lord God did something to confuse and terrorize the Amorites—no one knows what—and as they turned around to flee, He and the Israelites pursued them. Those of the enemy forces who weren't fast enough got killed by the sword. The others got hit by killer hailstones so discriminating that they didn't touch a single Israelite.

Even with God's help, the battle was long and arduous, and as the day progressed, Joshua realized he would need more time to bring about a decisive victory. There were still Amorites who had fled back toward their cities, and the five kings had hidden themselves in a cave at Makkedah. God wanted all of them vanquished; not one Amorite was to escape. Nightfall would only hamper the Israelites' progress, so Joshua made an astounding request—one engendered by a life lived in the sight of God and His wonders:

> Then Joshua spoke to the LORD in the day when the
> LORD delivered up the Amorites before the sons of
> Israel, and he said in the sight of Israel, "O sun, stand
> still at Gibeon, and O moon in the valley of Aijalon."
> So the sun stood still, and the moon stopped, until
> the nation avenged themselves of their enemies.
> Is it not written in the book of Jashar? And the sun
> stopped in the middle of the sky, and did not hasten
> to go down for about a whole day.
> And there was no day like that before it or after it,
> when the LORD listened to the voice of a man; for the
> LORD fought for Israel.
>
> JOSHUA 10:12-14

This was a miracle far greater than the parting of the Red Sea or the parting of the Jordan. No one knows how God accomplished this—whether the earth stopped turning on its axis so that the whole world experienced it, or God caused a light like the sun to continue shining in only that part of the world—but the fact is, although Moses and the Red Sea tend to get top billing among Bible stories, this was a wonder of wonders. The Israelites were on their feet for at least two full days considering their long trek up the mountain, but to witness God's miracles that day would have been worth the strain.

Note that Joshua did not take God aside and privately ask Him to hold the sun and the moon in their places, in case He should refuse his request. No, Joshua shouted it in the sight of all Israel. A key point in this scripture could easily be overlooked or misinterpreted:

> And there was no day like that before it or after it, when
> the LORD **listened** to the voice of a man...

This is not to say that the Lord doesn't normally listen to our voices. He listens very actively and very intently. But in this case, the word "listened" is "shâma" in Hebrew, and it actually means "to obey, to give heed." God *obeyed* the voice of Joshua. Joshua did not petition God to keep the sun shining; he simply shouted that it be so.

It would be wonderful to know the motivation behind such a statement. Was it simply wishful thinking on his part, just as we have been known to exclaim, "There aren't enough hours in a day!" Or was it a confident declaration emoting from the heart of a man who had seen God do awesome wonders for His people, and who had heard the LORD God Himself say that He was fighting for Israel? Perhaps God put the thought into his head. Whatever the case, Joshua declared it, and God made it happen.

So when the scripture says, *"And there was no day like that, before it or after it,"* it means that God doesn't usually respond to orders from us. A good dose of humility goes a long way. But Joshua was caught up in the heat of the moment, and God was proud of the valor of His ordained leader, and He might have said to Himself, "You got it, kid!"

There actually was a day similar to the day God made the sun stay in the sky. As the scripture at the beginning of this chapter relates, when King Hezekiah—who loved God—became ill, he asked God to heal him and give more years to his life. God spoke through the prophet Isaiah, and told Hezekiah that He would grant His request. Still, Hezekiah asked for a sign, and God offered him two options: He would either move the sun's shadow backward ten steps, or forward ten steps. Again, God was willing to mess with the cosmos.

King Hezekiah chose that it would move backward ten steps, because it was already in the process of moving forward anyway. The *Matthew Henry Complete Commentary on the Whole Bible* explains what happened this way:

> *It is supposed* that the degrees were half hours, and that it was just noon when the proposal was made, and the question is, "Shall the sun go back to its place at seven in the morning or forward to its place at five in the evening?' He humbly desired the sun might go back ten degrees, because, though either would be a great miracle, yet, it being the natural course of the sun to go forward, its going back would seem more strange, and would be more significant of Hezekiah's returning to the days of his youth (Job 33:25) and the lengthening out of the day of his life. It was accordingly

done, upon the prayer of Isaiah (v. 11): He cried unto the Lord by special warrant and direction, and God brought the sun back ten degrees, which appeared to Hezekiah (for the sign was intended for him) by the going back of the shadow upon the dial of Ahaz, which, it is likely, he could see through his chamber-window; and the same was observed upon all other dials, even in Babylon, 2 Chr. 32:31. Whether this retrograde motion of the sun was gradual or per saltum—suddenly—whether it went back at the same pace that it used to go forward, which would make the day ten hours longer than usual—or whether it darted back on a sudden, and, after continuing a little while, was restored again to its usual place, so that no change was made in the state of the heavenly bodies (as the learned bishop Patrick thinks)—we are not told; but this work of wonder shows the power of God in heaven as well as on earth, the great notice he takes of prayer, **and the great favour he bears to his chosen.**[2]

To reside in the favor of God's chosen is to live life as it was intended to be from the beginning: filled with happy, individualized gifts from the hand of our Father who delights in presenting them to us. Some are astonishing miracles; others are small expressions of love that are so obviously from heaven that they might as well have a tag attached to them saying, "Love, God."

Elijah was another of God's chosen—a prophet—and as God's mouthpiece, he witnessed amazing things. The only caveat to being one of God's chosen is that sometimes, you're very alone and very unpopular. God more than made up for Elijah's trials by keeping Elijah from death and escorting him to heaven in a fiery chariot (2 Kings 2:11).

One of Elijah's chief missions was to speak out against King Ahab, who was king over Israel, about his evil ways. He was another in a succession of evil kings who practiced idolatry and erected houses

---

[2]Henry, Matthew. "2 Kings 20." <u>Matthew Henry Commentary on the Whole Bible</u> (Complete). 2010. Crosswalk.com. 6 January 2010. http://www. crosswalk.com

for Baal, the male god of the Phoenicians and Canaanites. King Ahab was the son of King Omri, who is described as one who "walked in the way of Jeroboam." You'll remember the infamous Jeroboam, whose confrontation with the "man of God" in the preceding chapter resulted in the withering of his hand. There were several generations of kings between King Jeroboam and King Omri (Ahab's father), so being described as walking in the way of Jeroboam would be the same as comparing the president of the United States to Hitler. Not good.

Idolatry was firmly entrenched in the lifestyle of King Ahab, even though, amazingly, he was an Israelite, a member of God's chosen people.

> And Ahab the son of Omri did evil in the sight of the
> LORD more than all who were before him.
> 1 KINGS 16:30

The same was said earlier of Omri, so the evil of the kings became more and more pronounced. King Ahab then put the nail in his own coffin. He married Jezebel—an infamous name in all of literature. Her evil influence on Ahab and his kingdom made her name into an object of derision to this day.

> And it came about, as though it had been a trivial
> thing for him to walk in the sins of Jeroboam the son
> of Nebat, that he married Jezebel the daughter of Eth-
> baal king of the Sidonians, and went to serve Baal and
> worshipped him.
> 1 KINGS 16:31

Translation: As though it wasn't bad enough that King Ahab was doing the same things that Jeroboam had done, he topped it off by marrying Jezebel, whose father was the very icon of idolatry. Note his name: Ethbaal, which means "with Baal." God had specifically told the Israelites not to intermarry with the Canaanites:

"For they will turn your sons away from following Me
to serve other gods; then the anger of the LORD will be
kindled against you, and He will quickly destroy you."
DEUTERONOMY 7:4

With all of Joshua's conquests of Canaan, there were still cities and towns which had not been conquered by the time he died. Sidon, the hometown of King Ethbaal and his daughter Jezebel, was one of them. This was definitely not God's plan and He made his feelings clear to Joshua's successors:

> Now the angel of the LORD came up from Gilgal to
> Bochim. And he said, "I brought you up out of Egypt
> and led you into the land which I have sworn to your
> fathers; and I said, 'I will never break My covenant
> with you, and as for you, you shall make no covenant
> with the inhabitants of this land; you shall tear down
> their altars.' But you have not obeyed me; what is this
> you have done?
>
> "Therefore I also said, 'I will not drive them out
> before you; but they shall become as thorns in your
> sides, and their gods shall be a snare to you.'"
> JUDGES 2:1-3

During his reign King Ahab erected a house of Baal, an altar for Baal, and though it doesn't say so, one could assume an image of Baal. Ahab also built an Asherah, the female counterpart to Baal. Also during this time, a man named Hiel went about rebuilding the city of Jericho. This act was the equivalent of sticking his tongue out at God, because Joshua had specifically declared at the destruction of Jericho that anyone who should try to rebuild the city would lose his firstborn when laying the foundation, and his youngest when setting up the gates. Hiel experienced that exact fate. We can only surmise whether Hiel was influenced by King Ahab. Regardless, Israel had become a Godless nation.

So God summoned Elijah into service. Those dire times required a prophet of significance, endowed with enormous power. Elijah first came to Ahab's attention when he told him there would be a drought for years. It's hard to know whether Ahab took it seriously, but what we do know is that he told Jezebel. God knew the fury of Jezebel, and instructed Elijah to hide by a brook east of the Jordan. Jezebel decided to take matters into her own hands and destroyed as many of the prophets of the Lord as she could find, hoping eventually she'd unearth Elijah. Meanwhile, God had instructed ravens to bring Elijah bread and meat in the morning, and bread and meat in the evening.

Don't overlook this. *God instructed ravens to feed Elijah morning and night for weeks if not months.* Where did the bread and meat come from? Were these heavenly ravens? Our God of provision made it happen and that was that.

The drought that Elijah declared to Ahab was affecting everyone—even Elijah. Soon the stream that Elijah was drinking from dried up, and he was instructed to go into a town which was part of Sidon, because God said a widow would care for him there. When he found her, she was gathering sticks to make a fire to cook the last meal for herself and her son, because she had only a handful of flour left and a bit of oil. She expected to die not long after that last meal. Elijah then asked her to give *him* her last meal.

> Then Elijah said to her, "Do not fear; go, do as you have said, but make me a little bread cake from it first, and bring it out to me, and afterward you may make one for yourself and your son.
> "For thus says the LORD God of Israel, 'The bowl of flour shall not be exhausted, nor shall the jar of oil be empty, until the day that the LORD sends rain on the face of the earth.'"
> 1 KINGS 17:13-14

The widow was probably very thin after rationing her flour and oil for as long as possible. Now this was it—she couldn't put it off any longer. She was going to prepare their last meal and then wait to die.

Then comes Elijah—a stranger to her—asking her to give him the last meal. As a mother, she must have had a real mental struggle, because her first instinct would be to feed her child. How was she to know that Elijah was the real deal? He was the only prophet of God not in hiding, while the Baal prophets were as plentiful as lice.

The widow did as Elijah asked her, and there was plenty of flour and oil to feed all of them—for the next few years—because Elijah stayed with her until the end of the drought. Like the manna in the wilderness, the flour and the oil were there as long as they needed them. When the drought was over, and crops were able to grow again, the provision of flour and oil stopped. This wonder of God is not nearly so dramatic as some, but among the most tender. God, our provider, meets our needs.

It's interesting to note that when God sent Elijah to the suburb of Sidon, He was placing Elijah right under Jezebel's nose. She was still on her rampage, and would have given anything to get her hands on him. It was only when God decided to end the drought that he sent Elijah back to King Ahab. He found him in the midst of a search for what little grass was left so they could feed their livestock.

> And it came about, when Ahab saw Elijah that Ahab said to him, "Is this you, you troubler of Israel?"
>
> And he said, "I have not troubled Israel, but you and your father's house have, because you have forsaken the commandments of the LORD, and you have followed the Baals.
>
> "Now then send and gather to me all Israel at Mount Carmel, together with 450 prophets of Baal and 400 prophets of the Asherah, who eat at Jezebel's table."
> 1 KINGS 18:17-19

Elijah was asking King Ahab for a showdown between Ahab's gods, and the one true God. He wasn't about to end the drought until Ahab had it firmly fixed in his mind Who brought it on, and Who would end it. What followed was one of the most pictorial—and the most amusing—miracles in the Old Testament. Elijah had nothing if not an acid wit. He chose Mount Carmel, because, among other things, it was considered the special dwelling place of the gods.

> So Ahab sent a message among all the sons of Israel, and brought the prophets together at Mount Carmel.
> And Elijah came near to all the people and said, "How long will you hesitate between two opinions? If the LORD is God, follow Him; but if Baal, follow him." But the people did not answer him a word.

They didn't answer him because many—and probably most—had worshipped both God and Baal; the first, because it was in their tradition, and the second, to please Jezebel and to fit in with the culture of that society. They had played both sides of the ping-pong table and were on a wait-and-see status to see who they would align with.

> Then Elijah said to the people, "I alone am left a prophet of the LORD, but Baal's prophets are 450 men.
> "Now let them give us two oxen; and let them choose one ox for themselves and cut it up, and place it on the wood, but put no fire under it; and I will prepare the other ox, and lay it on the wood, and I will not put a fire under it.
> "Then you call on the name of your god, and I will call on the name of the LORD, and the God who answers by fire, He is God." And all the people answered and said, "That is a good idea."
> So Elijah said to the prophets of Baal, "Choose one ox for yourselves and prepare it first for you are many, and call on the name of your god, but put no fire under it."

Then they took the ox which was given them and they prepared it and called on the name of Baal from morning until noon saying, "O Baal, answer us." But there was no voice and no one answered. And they leaped about the altar which they made.

Nearly five hundred Baal prophets were leaping around for hours, trying to get Baal to do something. Elijah must have watched with undisguised amusement as Baal worshippers grew increasingly frantic. Eventually, he could keep silent no longer.

And it came about at noon, that Elijah mocked them and said, "Call out with a loud voice, for he is a god; either he is occupied or gone aside, or is on a journey, or perhaps he is asleep and needs to be awakened."

Was this moxie on Elijah's part or what? To egg on 450 Baal prophets was brazen, but God surely smiled at his impudence. It indicated that Elijah had a rock-solid belief that He was about to show up in blazing color.

So they cried with a loud voice and cut themselves according to their custom with swords and lances until the blood gushed out on them.

This so-called custom was against one of God's laws (Deut. 14:1), but they were so far removed from His word that they probably didn't know the difference.

And it came about when midday was past, that they'd raved until the time of the offering of the evening sacrifice; but there was no voice, no one answered, and no one paid attention.

Satan could very well have answered—and would have loved to—but God kept him under very tight surveillance during the debacle on Mount Carmel. In Revelation 13:13, it says:

> And he [Satan] performs great signs, so that he even makes fire come down out of heaven to the earth in the presence of men.

God ensured that He would be the only one to make His presence known, and He would do it in His usual awe-inspiring, all-consuming, pull-out-all-the-stops kind of style that makes front row seats the worst place to be.

But first, Elijah had to ensure that no one had any doubt in their minds that when God rained down His power, it was God and God alone.

> Then Elijah said to all the people, "Come near to me."

He wanted to show them there would be no sleight of hand.

> So all the people came near to him. And he repaired the altar of the LORD which had been torn down.
> And Elijah took twelve stones according to the number of the tribes of the sons of Jacob, [representing the 12 tribes of Israel] to whom the word of the LORD had come, saying, "Israel shall be your name."
> So with the stones he built an altar in the name of the LORD, and he made a trench around the altar, large enough to hold two measures of seed [approx. 22 quarts].
> Then he arranged the wood and cut the ox in pieces and laid it on the wood. And he said, "Fill four pitchers with water and pour it on the burnt offering and on the wood."

And he said, "Do it a second time," and they did it a second time. And he said, "Do it a third time," and they did it a third time.

And the water flowed around the altar, and he also filled the trench with water.

The altar, the wood and the ox were thoroughly drenched. No human could have started a fire if their life depended on it. And Elijah's life did depend on it, because if God did not answer him when he called, he would be torn limb from limb, or stoned or something similarly unsightly particularly after his bold-faced mockery of the 450 Baal prophets.

Then it came about at the time of the offering of the evening sacrifice, that Elijah the prophet came near and said, "O LORD, the God of Abraham, Isaac and Israel [God's name for Jacob], today let it be known that Thou art God in Israel, and that I am Thy servant, and that I have done all these things at Thy word.

"Answer me, O LORD, answer me, that this people may know that Thou, O LORD, art God, and that Thou hast turned their heart back again."

Then the fire of the LORD fell, and consumed the burnt offering and the wood and the stones and the dust, and licked up the water that was in the trench.

And when all the people saw it, they fell on their faces; and they said, "The LORD, He is God; the LORD, He is God."

1 KINGS 18:30-39

The fire of the Lord did not simply start atop the wood. The "fire of the Lord *fell.*" God Himself came down from heaven, for God is a consuming fire (Deut. 4:24). God has given Himself that description, and He reiterated it many times in the Old Testament.

The fire was so intense that even the stones were consumed, and the water in the trench. But note the one thing that was not touched in any way: the altar. What a mental picture: when the fire died down, everything was ash, except that blessed altar. That had to be preserved for future sacrifices to the Lord God. Baal was not to be worshipped in that place again, for God *"hast turned their heart back again."* Elijah stated the obvious even before God made His presence known. He knew that when God showed up, the Israelites' hearts would be turned back to Him.

God doesn't need to display such fantastic feats of His power. He's really quite secure in His own magnificence. He doesn't have to put on shows to make us "ooh" and "aah." But God will go to great lengths to turn our hearts back to Him. Or, like the Israelites and the pillar of fire, to keep our eyes on Him. Or, like the ravens for Elijah, to provide for us, His children.

It's what He does. It's who He is. It's how He loves.

Our God of wonders is performing small and large miracles all the time, every day. And there's always a purpose, and at the base of that purpose, is always, always, His faithful and abiding love.

Chapter 11

The Actively Present God

And He said, "My presence shall go with you, and I will give you rest." Then he [Moses] said to Him, "If Thy presence does not go with us, do not lead us up from here."

EXODUS 33:14-15

Moses knew God in the same way that we know our loved ones. God spoke to Moses face to face as a man speaks to his friend (Exodus 33:11), so Moses knew Him intimately and personally. Being in God's glorious presence is far more wonderful and possibly more *addicting* than being with anyone we know on earth. Many of us have experienced that kind of divine rapture in rare, fleeting moments, and when those moments are gone, we feel vaguely robbed and empty. Unfortunately, divine rapture is not something we can create on our own.

Whatever God's presence felt like, it was so thrilling that once he got a taste of it, Moses never wanted to be far from his God again. When God got angry at the Israelites after they had fashioned the golden calf and worshipped it, He told Moses that He had changed His mind—He would not be accompanying them to the Promised Land. He would send an angel with them instead.

Then the LORD spoke to Moses, "Depart, go up from here, you and the people whom you have brought up from the land of Egypt, to the land of which I swore to Abraham, Isaac, and Jacob, saying, 'To your descendants I will give it.'

"And I will send an angel before you and I will drive out the Canaanite, the Amorite, the Hittite, the Perizzite, the Hivite and the Jebusite.

"Go up to a land flowing with milk and honey; **for I will not go up in your midst**, because you are an obstinate people, lest I destroy you on the way."
EXODUS 33:1-3

When Moses heard this, he was desolate. *Anything* would have been a more welcome punishment. So Moses beseeched God to come with them, and presented a bold case which, had it been delivered by anyone else, might have merited a swift lightning bolt in the rear end.

Then Moses said to the LORD, "See, Thou dost say to me, 'Bring up this people!' But Thou Thyself hast not let me know whom Thou wilt send with me. Moreover, Thou hast said, 'I have known you by name, and you have also found favor in My sight.'

"Now therefore, I pray Thee, if I have found favor in Thy sight, let me know Thy ways, that I may know Thee, so that I may find favor in Thy sight. Consider too, that this nation is Thy people."
EXODUS 33:12-13

God had told Moses that He would send an angel with them, but Moses was so distraught, he didn't even hear the part about the angel accompanying them. All he'd heard was that God wasn't going with them, and everything after that was static. So he decided to play his one and only trump card: his favor with God.

Incidentally, when God said, "I have known you by name," it doesn't mean that He doesn't know each and every one of us by name. It means He had an intimate relationship with Moses because Moses had cultivated an intimate relationship with Him. He knew every one of those Israelites down to their DNA, but none had an intimate relationship with Him like their leader. Moses lived in what I like to call God's *active presence*.

What many people don't realize is that though God is *omnipresent*, He is not necessarily *actively* present. Everyone lives in God's omnipresence by default, whether they like it or not, but some, like Moses, choose to live in His active presence.

Why settle for God's usual when you could have His ultimate?

Moses practiced a style of living that relatively few people practice today, or even practiced during his time. That's because living in God's active presence requires actively seeking Him. It's a daily determination to go to God and cultivate a love relationship with Him.

The rewards of seeking God and living in His active presence are huge. When you live in God's active presence, you know He will set your feet on the right path—the *best* path for you. You see His gentle yet obvious hand in your life and you hear His still, small voice in your heart. When you live in God's active presence, you know He has a specific plan for your life, tailor-made to use your gifts and to bless you beyond imagining. You have a peace about things, and you look forward to the future with anticipation. Regardless of how old you are, if you live in God's active presence, you know you still have a purpose, and God still has treasures and surprises planned for your life, until He calls you home.

King David was another man who lived his life in God's active presence. He described it beautifully when he said:

> Thou wilt make known to me the path of life;
> In Thy presence is fullness of joy;
> In Thy right hand there are pleasures forever.
> Psalm 16:11

Fullness of joy. It means joy in its ultimate state. The presence of God is the ultimate thrill. Everything else pales in comparison. To David, God's presence was life itself. His life was entwined with God. Throughout the Psalms, David spoke of the joy of God's presence.

> For Thou dost make him most blessed forever;
> Thou dost make him joyful with gladness in Thy presence.
> PSALM 21:6

However, even though David had a sacred romance with God, he still had his humanity to contend with. When he committed his grievous sin of having sex with Bathsheba, and then issued the order that Bathsheba's husband be put on the front line of battle so that he was killed, he felt the heavy hand of God upon him. He knew he'd blown it and that God would punish him. God had high expectations of him, for David was king of Israel. He was willing to take whatever judgment God chose, but there was one thing David prayed fervently that God would not do:

> Do not cast me away from Thy presence,
> And do not take Thy Holy Spirit from me.
> PSALM 51:11

A painful separation

While David only feared being cast away from God's presence, Jesus actually experienced it. In fact, He actually experienced not only the terrifying absence of His Father's presence when He hung on the cross, but the actual *removal* of it. And since, as He once told His disciples, "I am in the Father, and the Father is in Me," the separation of God from Son of God must have felt quite literally like the ripping in half of the curtain that separated the holy place from the Holy of Holies in the temple.

> Now from the sixth hour [noon] darkness fell upon
> all the land until the ninth hour. And about the ninth
> hour Jesus cried out with a loud voice, saying, "Eli, Eli,
> Lama Sabachthani?" that is, "My God, My God, why
> hast thou forsaken Me?"
> MATTHEW 27:45-46

Throughout His life on earth, Jesus had not seen His Father, but He had felt His presence and had communed with Him through prayer. It was what sustained Him through more than thirty years away from His Father's side. But when He hung on the cross, and took on all the sins of mankind, God, Who is completely holy, had to withdraw Himself because He cannot be in the presence of sin. During those hours, God's beloved Son felt completely orphaned, and perhaps even cut in half.

Sadly, many people in the world will live their entire lives and never once feel His presence, or even care to. They don't realize that through His amazing grace, He makes the riches of Himself available to us if only we would ask Him. And He doesn't make it hard—He wants us simply to come looking.

> "As for you, my son Solomon, [David's son] know the
> God of your father, and serve Him with a whole heart
> and **a willing mind**; for the LORD searches all hearts,
> and understands every intent of the thoughts. **If you
> seek Him, He will let you find Him**; but if you forsake
> Him, He will reject you forever."
> 1 CHRONICLES 28:9

Why live life in a pup tent?

When you consider that the God of all that is—every planet and star, every galaxy and black hole—draws near to us at the first whisper of a heartfelt prayer, it is astounding to realize that many, many people don't even try to know Him. It's like being given the deed to the palace at Versailles, and never inserting the key in the lock, or going in to discover its treasures—treasures which are now yours—but instead, choosing to camp outside in a pup tent on the grass.

Those who live only in God's omnipresence may not think they're choosing anything at all. They don't even consider God as someone who wants to be involved with His creation. Most of these people store Him in a file in their head—in a file marked "Emergency"—and when a crisis arises, you can bet they're looking up His number.

That's because God implanted a need for Himself in our DNA. We were designed for daily, loving, respectful communication with our Creator—life lived in His active presence. When we choose to live that way, we have joy, peace, actual interaction with God through His internal voice, answers to prayer, a sense of purpose and surprisingly enough, an increasing hunger for His Word.

When we put God only in our "emergency" file—or no file at all—and live according to our own precepts and desires, we experience only what happens by natural circumstances. God lets the chips fall where they may, and probably won't shield us from the evil of the world or unexpected crises. In fact, if He knows that our hearts would respond to a jolt, He might just send a crisis our way to get our attention.

This is not to say that those who live in His active presence do not have crises—but the difference is, God has allowed those crises for a very specific purpose, and there's always a blessing on the other side:

> And we know that God causes all things to work to-
> gether for good to those who love God, to those who
> are called according to His purpose.
> Romans 8:28

Who's at your wheel?

The difference between a crisis in the life of someone who lives in God's active presence and someone who lives in His omnipresence is the difference between who's at the wheel. Those who put God at the wheel daily know that whatever He's allowing into your life is intended to get you to the destination He plans for you—*nothing* is happenstance. Those who insist on doing the driving have to fend for themselves.

For example, if a landslide suddenly occurs in front of the car that God is driving, the person inside can be assured that God probably wants to take him on a detour to a better place he never even dreamed of. If that same landslide occurs in front of the car that a person has driven without God, he will be frustrated and angry, and probably just turn around and head back to the very same place he started.

So how do we live in God's active presence? As stated in the verse on the preceding page, "If you seek Him, He will let you find him." We must first seek Him, and to do so, we must commit time to talk to Him. The beauty of our God is that He is available to us 24/7. He is always listening. Have you ever considered what a wonder that is? He is the only one in our lives Who is continually available to us—and even more amazing—longing for us to come to Him.

Once you establish a regular prayer life, you will begin to see answers to your prayers. He will also lead you to things that speak to concerns you may have. Let me illustrate.

As I write, my husband and I have been separated for a year. After 22 years of marriage, we were on a serious downward slide. We both needed a breather, and time to heal and forgive. Now, after untold hours of prayer, and by the sheer grace of God, my husband is moving back home and we are going to try to rebuild our marriage with God's help.

Although I know this is a God-won victory—I have felt a struggle with the devil over this marriage more than I have ever felt in my life—I am not yet tossing up confetti. Both my husband and I have a lot of trepidation about this because we don't want to repeat the behaviors we did in the past. And naturally, we're both afraid that our spouse is going to continue in habits that have historically rubbed us the wrong way.

What, your husband, too?

Last evening, I was alone in the house, because our children were at my husband's current house. I felt strongly that I needed some Biblical teaching since the trepidation was beginning to get the best of me, so I downloaded a favorite well-known Bible teacher teaching at a conference. Sometime into her session, she began to talk about her husband. She said that he could be very "carnal" at times, and that for years, she managed to get him to church about once a month. She also said that one moment he could use language that would curl her hair, and in the next moment pray over her in such a fashion that she could feel the Holy Spirit falling upon her. She couldn't figure it out: how could he be so carnal and yet so spiritual?

I sat there enrapt, so thankful for her transparency, and so glad to know that her husband is just as human as mine is. I knew then and there that the Lord had wanted me to hear that…to assure me that no one's husband is perfect…and that it's OK. (I'm sure my husband would be quick to inform my readers that I can be pretty carnal, too.)

God wanted to calm my heart, so He led me to that video, and because I live in God's active presence, I knew that He had orchestrated it for me. Actually, ever since my husband and I made the decision to move back in together a little over a week ago, God has been speaking loving words of encouragement to me in various forms: through unexpected calls from Christian friends, scripture that suddenly jumps out at me, and now this video.

This kind of communication with God is a thrill. Who else knows your heart the way He does, and delivers messages of love and encouragement exactly when you need them? Who else gives you answers that emerge from the most unlikely places, and give you the peace and assurance you so desperately crave?

God loves each and every person, but He rewards those who seek Him diligently with His amazing presence and a life that is filled with purpose, meaning, and untold blessings. It's the difference between walking through life in the dark, and walking in His light. Only when you know God and the sound of His voice, will you hear Him say, "This is the way, walk in it." (Isaiah 30:21).

Chapter 12

Our God Who Wounds

"Come, let us return to the LORD. For He has torn us, but He will heal us; He has wounded us, but He will bandage us. He will revive us after two days; He will raise us up on the third day that we may live before Him. So let us know, let us press on to know the LORD. His going forth is as certain as the dawn; and He will come to us like the rain, like the spring rain watering the earth."

HOSEA 6:1-3

Why would God want to wound us? There are many reasons, but God's ultimate intent in wounding us is to heal us and to save us.

God is like a wolf who tosses her pup into a river to save it from a forest fire. The pup will get swept away, tossed against some very sharp rocks, go under a few times and come up gasping for air, but he'll land downstream on a sandy bank, soaked, bruised, exhausted, but alive.

When God tosses us into the river, our immediate response is, "Why? What did I do to deserve this?" But God would much rather see us tossed in the river than burned in the fire. Most of the time, we can't see the fire that's burning right behind us, but God can. The forest fire may be something we've allowed into our lives that God knows will seriously burn us if we don't put it out: an affair, pornography, dabbling in the occult, illegal drug use, dishonest business practices, a gambling addiction, immorality...the list goes on.

This is why He wounds us so that He can heal us. Many who are thrown into the river have an epiphany once they've landed on the bank and caught their breath. They realize that life is uncertain, it can end at any time, they are not immortal, and they are not really in control of their lives after all.

> 'See now that I, I am He,
> And there is no god besides Me;
> It is I who put to death and give life,
> I have wounded, and it is I who heal;
> And there is no one who can deliver from My hand.'
> DEUTERONOMY 32:39

Wounding always slows us down and tends to invite introspection. We may have ignored God all of our lives, assuming we have all kinds of time to come to Him, but the end of our life may be coming much faster than we think. Wounding can give us that one opportunity that might have been lost had we run headlong over the metaphorical cliff of our lives, not even knowing our death was so near, and then suddenly face eternity without Him.

In the book, *Tuesdays with Morrie*, a younger man chronicles the last weeks of the life of his former professor, who has ALS (Lou Gehrig's Disease). Morrie, the professor, had always been an agnostic, but as the disease progressed to the point where Morrie knew his death was imminent, he, like so many others, began to acknowledge God.

Ted Koppel, who was host of the program "Nightline" at the time, had come to interview him a few times, and at his last interview, only a few weeks before his death, this is what Morrie said:

"Ted, this disease is knocking at my spirit. But it will not get my spirit. It'll get my body. It will not get my spirit."

Koppel was near tears. "You done good."

"You think so?" Morrie rolled his eyes toward the ceiling. "I'm bargaining with Him up there now. I'm asking Him, 'Do I get to be one of the angels?'"

It was the first time Morrie admitted talking to God.[1]

We cannot know what transpired between God and Morrie, or even if Morrie did the one thing God requires—accept His Son as Savior—but if he did, Morrie's wounding would have been successful.

He wouldn't, would He?

This is a hard and painful truth. Some people who read this will feel that they don't want to know a God who inflicts terrible diseases upon people. The fact is, I don't know if God inflicted the disease upon Morrie—He could have—or He could have simply *allowed* it. Either way, God's hand is involved. But you must realize this is the same God who, at the foundation of the world, planned that His beloved Son should die a terrible death for the redemption of the world. God NEVER wounds anyone just to watch them bleed. There is always a divine and perfect purpose with His immense love for us at the center of it. God's outlook is eternal; ours is about 60-80 years. He would rather Morrie suffer with ALS for a time and come home to Him, than go running headlong over the cliff into hell for his eternity.

Others receive wounds because of a sinful lifestyle.

> 'Why do you cry out over your injury?
> Your pain is incurable.
> Because your iniquity is great and your sins are numer-
> ous, I have done these things to you.'
> JEREMIAH 30:15

While this may sound harsh, it's important to know that when God wounds, He does not leave us there. He does what is necessary to get us to stop our sinful lifestyles, so that He can heal us. Note the following verse which follows the one above:

---

[1] Albom, Mitch. <u>Tuesdays with Morrie</u>. New York: Broadway Books, 2007.

> "For I will restore you to health and I will heal you of
> your wounds, declares the LORD…"
> JEREMIAH 30:17A

Look carefully at the order of these words. Why would God first restore us to health and then heal us of our wounds? Wouldn't we need to be healed of our wounds first before we can be restored to health? Not in God's economy.

Out of the pit

The word "restore" above is translated from the Hebrew word "âlâh" which means "to ascend; to mount up; to go up; to rise; to grow up; to be lifted up; to be put up; to be led up; to rise up." If we read the verse with this definition, it sheds a whole new light:

> "For I will restore you [raise you up, grow you up, lift
> you up, lead you up] to health and I will heal you of
> your wounds,' declares the LORD…"

What is he raising us up, or lifting us up, from? A pit of sin, most likely. God first wounds us to get our attention, then lifts us out of our pit of sin (restores us to health), and finally heals us.

This, once again, is a trust issue. A huge trust issue, in fact. We must trust that when we find ourselves wounded—when God allows unpleasant things to happen to us—it is for our greater good. When God wounds us, it is because He ultimately intends to heal us.

Incidentally, when God wants to lift us up out of our pit of sin, His wounding is not always physical. Sometimes it's a jab at our pride or our spirit. Or sometimes He will embarrass us, or cause us to be dishonored in front of others. I experienced this once about ten years ago.

I used to work part time out of our home as managing editor of a computer magazine. I loved the freedom it gave me. Occasionally, I would want to take a break, so I would cruise the internet. One day, I decided to see what kind of pornography I could pull up, and was shocked to see what was available with just the click of a button.

I went back to that same site a few times, drawn in by the same kind of titillation that has addicted so many thousands of people, especially men. Although I certainly was not at the point of addiction, I felt that I was adult enough to handle it. On about the third or fourth visit to the site, I was staring at a very unseemly picture when I received a phone call. It was from someone at my church. She wanted to talk about something regarding the Sunday School class I was teaching. Yep, you got it. The thought flashed through my mind that she would be shocked and disgusted to know what was on my screen at that moment.

I vowed not to go back to the site again, and didn't—for several weeks. But I couldn't resist, and visited the site one more time. I didn't receive another phone call, so I thought I'd gotten away with it. Then, a few days later, my husband told me he'd been checking the history on the computer, to make sure our young daughter wasn't visiting inappropriate sites. We didn't have a filter on our computer at that point—we do now. He asked me if I'd been the one to go to that unmentionable site. With embarrassment, I admitted that I had. I hadn't even been aware that my husband checked the history on our computers before that time.

God had "wounded" me again, but this time, the stakes had been higher, and He had really embarrassed me. I knew in my spirit that if I transgressed again, He would "up the stakes." I didn't want to take the chance to see what else He would do, so I quit visiting that site, and I haven't laid eyes on pornography since then.

There's an amusing postscript to that story. Not long ago, I was sitting in my car waiting for my daughter to emerge from her softball practice. As I waited, I cruised eBay on my laptop looking for fun decorative items to put in our vacation home which is a log cabin. I typed "log cabin" in the search space, and was paging through the different items when I saw that there was an old postcard with a nude woman in front of a log cabin. "What?" I thought, and clicked to make the tiny image larger. At that very moment, the battery on my computer went dead, and the computer shut off. The image never even had a chance to size up. I had to smile. And then I chuckled. God gives me very little leeway. But I love knowing that He cares so deeply for me and my holiness, and is so present in my life.

Sometimes God has to take drastic measures to turn His children around. In the nineteenth chapter of Isaiah, there is a message to Egypt about their idol worship. God tells them what He will do to Egypt to make them turn back to Him. The following verse sums it up:

> And the LORD will strike Egypt, striking but healing;
> so they will return to the LORD, and He will respond
> to them and will heal them.
> ISAIAH 19:22

Tough love

Wounding is a type of tough love. As a parent, I understand that because I've had to exercise a similar kind of tough love on my children.

When my daughter Christian was eleven, she wanted desperately to go to the concert of an enormously popular teen singer. She had never been to a concert like that, and Seattle happened to be the first venue of this singer's first concert tour. I bought the tickets for myself, Christian, and her best friend. Christian and her friend were beside themselves with excitement.

Christian's eleventh year was very trying for all of us. She was eleven going on sixteen, and her attitude was often snotty, disrespectful and downright rude. The sound of slamming doors had become common in our home. As the date for the concert approached, Christian seemed to be very secure in the knowledge that she would be going to the concert, regardless of her behavior, because the tickets had already been purchased.

One day, about a week before the concert, Christian was arguing vehemently with me about something. I told her to stop arguing and go up to her room. She continued to argue with me, so I got very close to her, looked her straight in the eye and said, "If you don't be quiet and go up to your room *right now*, you will not go to the concert. Do

NOT test me." Christian stubbornly stayed put and could not resist getting in the last word. To her utter shock and amazement, I declared that she had just forfeited her ticket to the concert.

Even though she headed to her room after that, Christian felt sure that I would not really follow through, particularly since my edict also meant her best friend would probably not be going to the concert—and I surely would not do that to her best friend.

As the days went by, and I did not change my mind, Christian began to realize that I meant business. As far as she was concerned, this was the concert of a lifetime, and I was visiting her "iniquity with stripes." She might as well have had forty lashes on her back. Her best friend wasn't thrilled with me either.

It was one of the hardest things I've had to do in disciplining my daughter. My heart absolutely broke for her, knowing how much it meant to her, but Christian needed a wake-up call. She needed to be wounded.

Eventually, she did get to see that pop star in concert. It was about a year and a half later that the same pop star came around in her second concert tour. But this time, it was attended by an older, wiser, and more respectful Christian. This time, not only did Christian mind her p's and q's, but her best friend and her best friend's mother reminded her weeks before the concert to behave herself, lest the same fate befall her again.

It's the same with God our loving heavenly Father. He doesn't want to inflict those kinds of stripes on us, but He will if He has to. He will visit our iniquity with stripes and we will feel the pain, but afterward, we will be wiser and humbler—and actually better for it.

A healing of the spirit

All of God's wounding does involve healing of some kind—if we will allow Him to heal us—but it is not always a physical healing. Jacob, in the book of Genesis, was physically wounded by God and never completely recovered—but he received a different kind of healing that he needed far more.

Jacob was the son of Isaac, who was the son of Abraham. When Isaac knew his death was drawing near, it was time to bestow the family blessing. The implications of this family blessing were huge: not only would the recipient of the blessing be served by his brothers, but his direct descendants would be the lineage through which "all the families of the earth" would be blessed in accordance with the covenant God made with Abraham.

Jacob had a twin brother Esau, and Isaac favored Esau, so he fully intended to give the blessing to Esau. Furthermore, Esau was the first out of the womb, although Jacob was grasping his heel, so he came out right behind. Isaac's wife Rebekah favored Jacob, and when she learned of Isaac's intention to give Esau the blessing, she concocted a plan to help Jacob get the family blessing. Isaac's sight was nearly gone, so Jacob pretended to be Esau and swindled Isaac into giving him the blessing.

Esau knew that Isaac was intending to give him the blessing, and when he found out that Jacob had stolen the blessing that belonged to him, Esau wanted to kill him. Rebekah told Jacob to flee to her brother, Laban, and stay with him until Esau's anger subsided.

On his way to his Uncle Laban's home, God appeared to Jacob in a dream, and told him that He would be with him. Even though Jacob had stolen the blessing, God honored the blessing of Isaac, and promised that Jacob would carry on the sacred lineage begun by Abraham through which Jesus, the Savior of the world, would be born. Throughout Jacob's life, God's grace and forgiveness was clearly evident, for Jacob did not deserve the blessing or the visitation of God. Still, God did not let him get off easily for his trickery. He would end up paying a high price for his dishonesty by meeting up with someone who would repay him in kind.

I married who?

Jacob was a schemer, apparently arriving at such tendencies through the influence of his mother, but he met his match with his uncle Laban. Not long after Jacob arrived at Laban's house, he fell in love with Laban's daughter, Rachel, and asked for her hand in marriage. When Laban saw how much Jacob loved Rachel, he declared that Jacob had to work for him for seven years before he could marry Rachel. Jacob did so, and when finally his wedding night arrived, Laban secretly put his daughter Leah, Rachel's sister, in Jacob's marriage bed instead of Rachel. Jacob must have left the light off, because when he awoke in the morning, he was shocked to find that he had consummated his marriage with the wrong woman. Laban then declared that Jacob had to work another seven years to win Rachel for his wife.

Jacob agreed, and Laban gave Rachel to him so that Jacob did not have to wait for her for another seven years. Jacob actually worked for Laban another 13 years, and amassed a stunning flock of livestock and enviable wealth. Consistent with Jacob's character, he did so in a rather underhanded way.

Laban's sons began accusing Jacob of using their father to accumulate all his wealth. God then came to Jacob in a dream and told him to go back to Bethel, his homeland—the place God promised to give to him and his descendants. God may have seen that if Jacob didn't leave, he might have met with the consequences of Laban's sons' anger. Jacob packed up his two wives and children, and caravanned with his huge herds of livestock and servants back to the country of Edom, where he knew he would have to face his brother Esau.

Esau and 400 close friends

As he drew closer to Esau's town, he began to fear how his brother would react. He fell to scheming again, and devised a plan that would hopefully curry his brother's favor before he laid eyes on him. He sent messengers a few days ahead to advise Esau that he was coming, and to get a feel for his reaction. The messengers returned and said that Esau was coming to meet him—with 400 men. Jacob's face went white at the news.

So he divided the people and livestock who were with him into two companies, and sent them in separate groups, one ahead of the other, so that if Esau attacked the first company, the other would be spared. He also sent with those companies a huge offering of livestock and servants to present to his brother as a gift.

Just in case that wasn't enough to appease Esau, Jacob sent his two wives, maids and children ahead of him, after the offering of livestock and servants, hoping to soften his heart at the sight of them.

Jacob helped his wives and children across the Jabbok River, then came back across the river. Jacob had placed a lot of insurance between himself and his brother—the last being the river itself. Did it ever occur to him that he was not so much crafty as cowardly, not seeming to care if his brother attacked the first company of people and killed them, or possibly even the second company, and his wives and children as well?

That night as Jacob was anticipating what might happen the next day, a man appeared to him and wrestled with him until daybreak. (Genesis 32:24) There is no explanation as to why the man appeared or began wrestling with him, but after wrestling with him *all night long*, and not being able to defeat Jacob, the visitor touched the socket of Jacob's thigh, and dislocated it, but still, Jacob continued to wrestle.

> Then he [the visitor] said, "Let me go, for the dawn is breaking." But he [Jacob] said, "I will not let you go unless you bless me."
>
> So he said to him, "What is your name?" And he said, "Jacob."
>
> And he said, "Your name shall no longer be Jacob, but Israel; for you have striven with God and with men and have prevailed."
>
> GENESIS 32:27-28

The wrestling opponent of his dreams

Could Jacob have been wrestling with God Himself? Jacob thought so, for he named the place where he wrestled with the man, "Peniel," which means "face of God," because he said, "I have seen God face to face, yet my life has been preserved." (Genesis 32:30)

It would be so like our God to know that deep in Jacob's spirit, he had never felt worthy of the blessing he stole from his brother. All his life, he had lived up to the meaning of his name which is "supplanter," meaning "to supersede another especially by force or treachery."[2] God knew he needed an opportunity to earn a real, bona fide blessing on his own merit, without using his cunning or dishonest means. So the Lord God took Jacob on in hand-to-hand combat. Of course God could have beaten him. But the Lord God apparently appeared in the same stature and strength of Jacob, so they could have an honest fight.

Can you imagine what went through Jacob's head? He was wrestling with the Lord God Himself! What a thrill! Perhaps God even offered Jacob a blessing if he won. Surely that was why Jacob's adrenaline was running so fast and furious that he was still going strong at daybreak. You can be sure as he fought against the Lord that he was already formulating the words he would say to his brother Esau and everyone else who would listen, "You'll never guess who I wrestled with last night…God…yeah, God! Seriously, I did!"

It's hard to tell who won, or even if there was a victor. All the Bible says is that the heavenly visitor saw that He did not prevail against Jacob, i.e., He did not gain the upper hand, and therefore dislocated the socket of his thigh to show him who had preeminence. With that wounding, Jacob gained some much-needed humility, and limped for the rest of his life.

But God healed him in another, far more important way. God knew Jacob needed a new name, a name that would denote that he had finally earned an honest blessing, and now had a reason to hold his head high. So He gave him the name "Israel" which means "he who strives with God." The word "strive" means to "devote serious effort or energy."

Beautiful semantics

Did you notice the way God phrased Jacob's new name? The key word in "he who strives with God" is the word "with." Isn't it interesting how God can look at things? God said that Jacob had striven

---

[2]Mish, Frederick C., ed. in chief. <u>Merriam Webster's Collegiate Dictionary</u>. Springfield, Mass: Merriam-Webster, Incorporated, 1993.

"with" Him, not "against" Him. And wouldn't you want to be known as someone who "devoted serious effort and energy *with* God?" Wouldn't you just beam if God gave you such a name?

That was the real blessing God gave Jacob that day; the real healing of his heart and his self esteem. Perhaps God dislocated his socket to give him a war wound of sorts, something tangible that proved he did, indeed, wrestle with God. Jacob's new name was also pivotal in another way. "Israel" went on to have twelve sons who became the twelve tribes of Israel, so Jacob's new name also became the name of the huge nation of Israel that would be known as...God's chosen people.

It's no wonder that after this, Jacob was a changed man. Although he had planned to be the last to face his brother, when he came within sight of Esau, Jacob *ran* ahead of his wives and children—even with a limp—and bowed down to the ground seven times before he reached his brother. This gesture of humility was certainly not easy with the pain of a dislocated hip.

> Then Esau ran to meet him and embraced him, and
> fell on his neck and kissed him, and they wept.
> GENESIS 33:4

All of Jacob's scheming had been for nothing. God had changed Esau's heart and Jacob's as well. We must trust that when God wounds us, He means ultimately to heal us. In Jacob's case, he wounded his hip but healed his heart and his relationship with his twin brother.

If you are being wounded, torn, purged, purified or refined, consider yourself blessed. God considers you worthy of His attention and wants to heal something in your life that may have been causing problems for years. It may be something you didn't even know required healing. For me, it has been a need for control and dominance. (This is certainly not my only issue, but at this writing, it is the one He has taken to task.) For you, it may be anxiety, fear, an addiction to things like shopping, the internet or pornography, or it could be deep-seated anger or resentment.

If you have had God on the back burner all your life—or barely even acknowledged Him—your wounding may be His attempt to save your soul. If you're currently bleeding profusely with a certain kind of wounding, don't make the mistake of getting mad at God. Hard as it may be, thank Him for His loving diligence to you. If you let Him, He will work this out for your good. Just let the surgeon do His work. He knows what He's doing.

Chapter 13

The Glory of Our God

"I am the LORD, that is My name; I will not give my
glory to another, nor my praise to graven images."
ISAIAH 42:8

God's glory is what makes God, God. It is His essence.
All glory emanates from God. Nothing and no one can create their own
glory. Even God's beloved Son, Jesus, derives His glory from His Father:

Jesus answered, "If I glorify Myself, My glory is nothing; it is My Father who glorifies Me..."
JOHN 8:54

So what is God's glory? Most people tend to think of God's glory
in a visual sense. God's visual glory, which I like to call His *radiant*
glory, is almost always accompanied with a cloud, the brilliance of a
consuming fire, and sometimes sheer radiance. However, God's radiant glory is only one facet of His glory. God's glory is actually like a
multi-faceted diamond, because there are many beautiful—and practical—sides to it. It is multi-dimensional and multi-purpose. Since His
radiant glory is the facet we most easily associate with His glory, let's
explore that first.

The first recorded display of God's glory was witnessed by Abraham when God made the covenant with him that established him as the father of a new nation—a nation that would be called God's chosen people, Israel.

A covenant is usually a solemn, binding agreement between two parties, but this particular covenant was a promise made by God, and Abraham and his descendants would be the beneficiaries. Because only God could guarantee the covenant's fruition, He performed the traditional covenantal ceremony by Himself, and when He did so, He sealed it with His glory.

> And He said to him [Abraham], "I am the LORD who brought you out of Ur of the Chaldeans, to give you this land to possess it."
>
> And he said, "O LORD GOD, how may I know that I shall possess it?"
>
> So He said to him, "Bring Me a three year old heifer, and a three year old female goat, and a three year old ram, and a turtledove, and a young pigeon."
>
> Then he brought all these to Him and cut them in two, and laid each half opposite the other; but he did not cut the birds.
>
> And the birds of prey came down upon the carcasses, and Abram drove them away.
>
> Now when the sun was going down, a deep sleep fell upon Abram; and behold, terror and great darkness fell upon him.
>
> And God said to Abram, "Know for certain that your descendants will be strangers in a land that is not theirs, where they will be enslaved and oppressed four hundred years.
>
> "But I will also judge the nation whom they will serve; and afterward they will come out with many possessions.
>
> "And as for you, you shall go to your fathers in peace; you shall be buried at a good old age."

And it came about when the sun had set, that it was very dark, and behold, there appeared a smoking oven and a flaming torch which passed between these pieces.

On that day the LORD made a covenant with Abram, saying,

"To your descendants I have given this land, from the river of Egypt as far as the great river, the river Euphrates: the Kenite and the Kenizzite and the Kadmonite and the Hittite and the Perizzite and the Rephaim and the Amorite and the Canaanite and the Girgashite and the Jebusite."

GENESIS 15:7-15, 17-21

Sealing His promise with His glorious presence

God and His glory actually passed between the pieces! This is both awe-inspiring and gruesome at the same time. Visualize the incredible scene. While the use of cut-up animals seems very gory, God was actually carrying out an ancient Eastern manner of making a covenant:

…both the contracting parties passed through the divided pieces of the slain animals, thus symbolically attesting that they pledged their very lives to the fulfillment of the engagement they made (see Jer. 34:18, 19). Now in Genesis 15, God alone, whose presence was symbolized by the smoking furnace and lamp of fire, passed through the midst of the pieces of the slain animals, while Abraham was simply a spectator of this wonderful exhibition of God's free grace.[1]

Abraham, completely overcome by the very presence of God, could only watch as God Himself passed between the slain animals. It was very dark, and out of the darkness appeared something Abraham could hardly put into words. God looked like a "smoking oven," often

---

[1]McDonald, William. "Genesis." Farstad, Art, ed. Believer's Bible Commentary. Nashville, TN: Thomas Nelson Publishers, 1995, quoting David Baron, The New Order of the Priesthood, pp. 9-10 footnote.

referred to in other passages as a "smoking furnace," and a flaming torch. Others who have seen God have described Him in a similar fashion in other scriptures, with equally inept word pictures:

> In the midst of the living beings there was something that looked like burning coals of fire, like torches darting back and forth among the living beings. The fire was bright, and lightning was flashing from the fire.
> EZEKIEL 1:13

Ezekiel was describing his vision of God in the middle of the cherubim (the living beings). Now look at how Christ is described in Daniel (Old Testament) and in Revelation (New Testament):

> His body also was like beryl, his face had the appearance of lightning, his eyes were like flaming torches, his arms and feet like the gleam of polished bronze, and the sound of his words like the sound of a tumult.
> DANIEL 10:5-6

> And His head and His hair were white like white wool, like snow; and His eyes were like a flame of fire; and His feet were like burnished bronze, when it has been caused to glow in a furnace, and His voice was like the sound of many waters.
> REVELATION 1:14-15

These descriptions were penned about 600 years apart, yet the similarities are striking. The glorified Christ Jesus appears with fire in His eyes like a flaming torch, just like the flaming torch of God that appeared when He cut the covenant with Abraham.

Words fail to describe just how magnificently terrifying the covenant scene was. Abraham's response was a deep sleep, and the sensation of terror and great darkness. Abraham may have fainted, and in the midst of that twilight world, he experienced terror and great darkness. This was a common response among those who witnessed

God's glory. This must be the fear of God in its purest form—the body's response to the presence of the holy and magnificent God. It doesn't say specifically, but God must have set Abraham on his feet, just as He did with others in similar situations.

Holy terror

Daniel also fell into a deep sleep while in the midst of a heavenly vision:

> And I heard the voice of a man between the banks of Ulai, and he called out and said, "Gabriel, give this man an understanding of the vision."
>
> So he came near to where I was standing, and when he came I was frightened and fell on my face; but he said to me, "Son of man, understand that the vision pertains to the time of the end."
>
> Now while he was talking with me, I sank into a deep sleep with my face to the ground; but he touched me and made me stand upright.
> DANIEL 8:16-18

When Daniel saw Christ and described Him (as noted on the previous page) not only was he seized with terror, but also the people who stood nearby, even though they saw or heard nothing. The very presence of the glory of God, even if not seen or heard, is still palpable and terrifying:

> Now I, Daniel, alone saw the vision, while the men who were with me did not see the vision; nevertheless, a great dread fell on them, and they ran away to hide themselves.
>
> So I was left alone and saw this great vision; yet no strength was left in me, for my natural color turned to a deathly pallor, and I retained no strength.

> But I heard the sound of the words; and as soon as
> I heard the sound of his words, I fell into a deep sleep
> on my face, with my face to the ground.
> Daniel 10:7-9

The men who stood with Daniel threw their bravado to the wind and ran. Daniel ended up flat on his face—in a posture of worship, whether he intended to or not—just like all the others who witnessed God's glory first-hand. We are meant to worship; our bodies were designed for such a purpose. Just as we are forced to blink when we sneeze, we are guaranteed to go prostrate in God's holy presence.

Each time one of the prophets or disciples fell at the sight of God's glory, God, the Lord Jesus, or one of the holy angels quickly told them to stand on their feet, for God did not want to address the back of their heads. Since it's impossible to stand in the presence of God, heavenly help is usually required.

> Then He said to me, "Son of man, stand on your feet
> that I may speak with you!"
> And as He spoke to me the Spirit entered me and
> set me on my feet; and I heard Him speaking to me.
> Ezekiel 2:1-2

When Ezekiel faced God a second time, again he was assisted to his feet:

> The Spirit then entered me and made me stand on my
> feet, and He spoke with me...
> Ezekiel 3:24

And when John, the beloved disciple was taken to heaven and beheld Jesus in His glorified form, He found himself on the ground like all of the others. Jesus laid His hand upon John, and enabled him to stand:

> And when I saw Him, I fell at His feet like a dead man.
> And He laid His right hand upon me, saying, "Do not
> be afraid, I am the first and the last, and the living One;
> and I was dead, and behold, I am alive forevermore,
> and I have the keys of death and of Hades."
> REVELATION 1:12-18

The power of glory

God's radiant glory is not merely light. It is even more than a consuming fire. It is a force that cannot be reckoned with. "Power and glory" are often spoken together in the Bible, inferring that glory does not occur without power. When God appeared in His glory, He was usually accompanied by a "storm wind," "the earth quaking," and thunder and lightning. If people didn't get down on their faces, they went down.

Incidentally, the glory displayed atop Mount Sinai was not God's full glory. The fact that the Israelites could witness such a display and live indicates that God did not show it to them unedited. The aftermath of His full glory would look something like Hiroshima after the fall of the atom bomb or Mt. St. Helens when it blew—sheer unbridled power and energy. Habakkuk describes what happens when God does not set boundaries on His glory:

> He stood and surveyed the earth;
> He looked and startled the nations.
> Yes, the perpetual mountains were shattered,
> The ancient hills collapsed.
> His ways are everlasting.
> HABAKKUK 3:6

He looked and startled the nations. With God's glory unveiled, He has only to look at the world, and He will startle the nations—all of them, all at the same time. We're talking *the whole world,* dropping to its knees. Can you imagine a sudden burst of light so intense, so penetrating, that all you can do is drop to the ground and shield your face with your arms?

For the record, that *will* happen one day.

> "But immediately after the tribulation of those days the sun will be darkened, and the moon will not give its light, and the stars will fall from the sky, and the powers of the heavens will be shaken, and then the sign of the Son of Man will appear in the sky, and then all the tribes of the earth will mourn, and they will see the Son of Man coming on the clouds of the sky with power and great glory.
>
> "And He will send forth His angels with a great trumpet and they will gather together His elect from the four winds, from one end of the sky to the other."
> MATTHEW 24:29-31

Worldwide glory

How is it that the entire world will see the Son of Man—Jesus—appearing in the sky with power and great glory? Not even the sun can be seen by the entire world at one time. Well, as it states, "the powers of the heavens will be shaken." Jesus' glory will be so intense that it will darken the sun, robbing the moon of its light, and dislodging the stars from their resting places. All the tribes, i.e. peoples, of the earth will mourn from sheer terror and the realization that they did not give heed to the call of God in their hearts. They will be so terrified at the appearance of Jesus' glory that they will ask the mountains to fall upon them.

And the kings of the earth and the great men and the commanders and the rich and the strong and every slave and free man, hid themselves in the caves and among the rocks of the mountains; and they said to the mountains and to the rocks, "Fall on us and hide us from the presence of Him who sits on the throne, and from the wrath of the Lamb; for the great day of their wrath has come; and who is able to stand?"

Revelation 6:15-17

This will be Jesus in full glory, and indeed, no one will be able to stand. Everyone will be driven to their knees, or flat on their face. And they will be saying things they never thought would issue from their lips.

"I have sworn by Myself,
The word has gone forth from My mouth in righteousness
And will not turn back,
That to Me every knee will bow, every tongue will swear allegiance.
"They will say of Me, 'Only in the Lord are righteousness and strength.'
Men will come to Him,
And all who were angry at Him shall be put to shame."

Isaiah 45:23-24

Paul reiterated this same concept in his letter to the Philippians:

Therefore also God highly exalted Him, and bestowed on Him the name which is above every name, that at the name of Jesus every knee should bow, of those who are in heaven, and on earth, and under the earth, and that every tongue should confess that Jesus Christ is Lord, to the glory of God the Father.

PHILIPPIANS 2:9-10

God's glory: the truth serum

This confession of Christ as Lord will not be voluntary, but rather involuntary. Just as our hearts beat involuntarily, so will our tongues speak the truth about Christ when we behold His glory. Whether Christians, Jews, on-the-fencers, agnostics or atheists—everyone will say, "Jesus Christ is Lord!" when met with His glory, without even realizing it.

This is a truth that is imbedded deep within our souls—a knowledge that we were made for a personal relationship with our Heavenly Father, and that He alone can save. Why else do people who have ignored Him all their lives try to bargain with Him when they are faced with their mortality? "Oh, my God!" many of them have said without thinking all their lives, and when they behold Him, they will fall on their faces, and there will be no doubt Whom they are beholding. Not once will anyone say, "Oh Buddha!" or "Oh Baal!" or "Oh Asherah!"

This is another facet of God's radiant glory: it inspires instantaneous truth. When Paul talked about every knee bowing before the Lord, and every tongue confessing that Jesus Christ is Lord, he was speaking from personal experience. Before he was an apostle, he was a zealous and powerful persecutor of the early church. But then the Lord Jesus gave him a shot of full-on glory that forever changed him:

> And it came about that as he journeyed, he was approaching Damascus, and suddenly a light from heaven flashed around him; and he fell to the ground, and heard a voice saying to him, "Saul, Saul, why are you persecuting Me?"
>
> And he said, "Who art Thou, Lord?" And He said, "I am Jesus whom you are persecuting, but rise, and enter the city, and it shall be told you what you must do."

> And the men who traveled with him stood speechless, hearing the voice, but seeing no one.
>
> And Saul got up from the ground, and though his eyes were open, he could see nothing; and leading him by the hand, they brought him into Damascus.
>
> ACTS 9:3-8

Saul (later called Paul) dropped to the ground, just like the rest of those who have witnessed God's glory. Paul also knew instinctively who was speaking to him, even before Jesus identified Himself. He'd never met Jesus in person, and Jesus had already ascended back into heaven. He'd heard of Jesus, and through the preaching of Stephen, he'd been told that Jesus had risen from the dead, but Paul's zeal to destroy the early church made it clear he didn't believe it. Yet his immediate, involuntary response was, "Who are Thou, Lord?" The Greek word which Paul used for "Lord" was "*Kurios,*" which means, "Lord, wielding authority for good." The Lord's glory gave Paul instantaneous truth, so that he knew that the One speaking to him was Lord, that He was innately good, and was wielding His authority.

The immediate and involuntary confession of God's or Jesus' identity by people when met with His glory often went hand in hand with a declaration of His goodness. Like Paul, Solomon and his priests had a similar response:

> Now when Solomon had finished praying, fire came down from heaven and consumed the burnt offering and the sacrifices; and the glory of the LORD filled the house. And the priests could not enter into the house of the LORD, because the glory of the LORD filled the LORD's house.
>
> And all the sons of Israel, seeing the fire come down and the glory of the LORD upon the house, bowed down on the pavement with their faces to the ground, and they worshipped and gave praise to the LORD, saying, "Truly He is good, truly His lovingkindness is everlasting."
>
> 2 CHRONICLES 7:1-3

Somehow, when viewing God's glory, it is immediately apparent that God is good. It would seem that Solomon and the priests would say something more like, "Wow, God is amazing. Look at that!" But what they said was, "Truly He is good."

God's glory, then, is also His goodness in visual form.

Consider the amazing love scene between Moses and God atop Mt. Sinai. After long weeks spent together as God dictated His laws and Moses scribed them, Moses began to feel an intimacy and a comfort with his God. One day, Moses blurted something from the absolute depths of his soul:

"I pray thee, show me Thy glory!"

Moses had already seen God's glory in blazing brilliance, so what was he asking? Moses knew, at the base of his soul, there was so much more to God. He wanted to go deeper. So he asked—and God gladly responded:

> And He said, "I Myself will make all My goodness pass before you, and will proclaim the name of the LORD before you; and I will be gracious to whom I will be gracious, and will show compassion on whom I will show compassion."
>
> But He said, "You cannot see My face, for no man can see Me and live!"
>
> EXODUS 33:19-20

Oh His goodness!

It's hard to imagine what "goodness" in its purest form looks like, but it is apparently so brilliant that it cannot be looked upon with human eyes. But if you think about all of God's goodness—the results of what we can see here on this Earth—concentrated into a few moments of indefinable splendor, it's easy to understand why it was more brilliance than Moses could take. Charles Haddon Spurgeon, a renowned English preacher in the second half of the nineteenth century, described why God's goodness is far too vast to contain in a fleeting vision:

> There is a panorama such as time would not be long enough for you to see. Consider the goodness of God in creation. Who could ever tell all God's goodness there? Why, every creek that runs up into the shore is full of it where the fry dance in the water. Why, every tree and every forest rings with it; where the feathered songsters sit and make their wings quiver with delight and ecstasy. Why, every atom of this air, which is dense with animalculae, is full of God's goodness. The cattle on a thousand hills he feeds; the ravens come and peck their food from his liberal hands. The fishes leap out of their element, and he supplies them; every insect is nourished by him. The lion roars in the forest for his prey, and he sendeth it to him. Ten thousand thousand creatures are all fed by him. Can you tell, then, what God's goodness is? If you knew all the myriad works of God, would your life be long enough to make all God's creative goodness pass before you?[2]

When God passed His goodness in front of him, He put Moses in the cleft of a rock, and covered him with His hand, so that the intensity did not sear his eyes to blindness, nor burn his skin to leather. Knowing that Moses could not look upon him, God graciously described Himself—the essence of goodness—as He passed by:

> "The LORD, the LORD God, compassionate and gracious, slow to anger, and abounding in lovingkindness and truth; who keeps lovingkindness for thousands, who forgives iniquity, transgression and sin; yet He will by

---

[2]Spurgeon, Charles. A View of God's Glory. 1908. The Spurgeon Archive. 15 January 2010 <http://www.spurgeon.org/sermons/3120.htm>

no means leave the guilty unpunished, visiting the iniquity of fathers on the children and on the grand-children to the third and fourth generations."
EXODUS 34:6-7

We've seen that God's glory is a purifying consuming fire, His goodness in visual form, something that invokes absolute truth, and humbles all who witness it.

Glory emanates and *originates* from God only. Therefore, when God says, *"I am the LORD, that is My name; I will not give my glory to another, nor my praise to graven images,"* it is not an issue of ego, it is an issue of identity. The word "glory" in this verse comes from the Hebrew word, *"kâbôwd"* or *"kâbôd,"* meaning, "weight, honor, esteem, majesty, abundance, wealth." God and His glory are one and the same. If God gave His glory to another, He would no longer be God, in the same way that if you gave your personality to another, you would no longer be you.

The inner beauty of bestowed glory

Although God will not give anyone *His* glory—and rightfully so—God delights in glorifying His beloved. This is another kind of glory, one I like to call *bestowed* glory. God can and does confer glory to those whom He loves, but He does not subtract from His own glory. This might seem like an issue of semantics, but it's an important point. Consider how the sun sheds its light or its "glory" on the earth and the moon without giving any of its own glory away. If it did give away of itself, it would slowly diminish, and no longer be the sun that we know and appreciate for its warmth.

In a similar fashion, God bestows glory upon His Son Jesus, and likewise, His Son bestows glory upon us. Shortly before Jesus was to be arrested in the Garden of Gethsemane, Jesus prayed what has become known as His "High Priestly Prayer," in which He interceded for His disciples and all those in the ages to come who would claim Him as their Savior:

> "And the glory which Thou hast given Me I have given
> to them; that they may be one, just as We are one; I in
> them, and Thou in Me, that they may be perfected in
> unity, that the world may know that Thou didst send
> Me, and didst love them, even as Thou didst love Me."
> JOHN 17:22-23

The word "glory" in the verses above is a different kind of glory than the one used for God. It is derived from a Greek word, "*doxa*," which, among its meanings is, "not the outward glorious appearance, attracting attention to the person or thing itself, but that glory shown from within reflecting in the appearance which attracts attention." The predominating meaning of "*doxa*" is "recognition." Jesus had given the disciples an inner glory, something that differentiated them as His followers. They would be "one," having that same inner glory, just as Jesus and His Father were one, because *He* was in them, just as God was in Jesus.

When Jesus prayed this prayer, He was nearing the end of His ministry in the world, and the training period with His disciples. He was progressing from there to the Garden of Gethsemane, and then to His crucifixion. After He was raised from the dead, it would be only 40 days before He ascended into heaven. He wanted to leave something of Himself in the world so that it could see Him still visibly present in His disciples. So He gave some of His glory to His disciples, so that the world would know that He truly was the Son of God, and that God had sent Him.

I believe that Christians through the ages have had, and presently do have, that same glory. I believe that the glory Jesus conferred upon His disciples—and those who would subsequently follow Him through the ages—was something that could be recognized by non-Christians. It is a kind of inner glow, clearly emanating from Jesus, whose source is God.

A few years ago, something interesting happened when I walked into a Starbucks coffee shop. As I got in line, a man ahead of me picked up his drink, said "thank you" to the barista, and walked out. I never saw his face. But something about him immediately attracted my attention—I can't even put my finger on what it was—and I turned to look at him. As I watched him leave, I knew without a doubt that he was a Christian, and not a new Christian, but a giant in the faith. I felt almost like John the Baptist had just passed by. There was a kind of glory that emanated from him. It was instantaneous recognition, even from behind!

Jesus bestows God's glory upon us for two reasons:

> "[1]…that they may be perfected in unity, [2] that the world may know that Thou didst send Me, and didst love them, even as Thou didst love Me."

God's 3-D glory glasses

As Christ stated, God's glory creates unity, and this is yet another characteristic of His glory. When God's glory radiates from within a believer, the external fades away, and we begin to see others the way Christ sees us, thus unifying us. It's like we put on 3-D glasses, and all the inner beauty and God-given gifts of a person suddenly appear. We no longer see our external "differences;" we see each other's gifts, and how we each are uniquely gifted for the purpose of contributing to the body of believers, and to the world at large.

I was recently at a gathering of women at my church. One of the women was asked to stand up and speak. She is an immigrant from an Asian country, and before she spoke, she apologized that English is her second language, and that she might stumble a bit. Then she began to speak, straight from her heart. Within minutes, we were all astounded at her gift of preaching. The glory of God began to shine brightly through her, and we all saw her in a beautiful new way. God's glory shining through her took her from ordinary to extraordinary: a woman gifted by God to preach and *preach with power*.

As believers, we are the only conduit through which God's glory can shine. It is God's glory *in us* that gives others a glimpse of Him.

Some time ago, I was on a plane, flying home to Seattle from Las Vegas, where I'd gone to visit a friend. She actually lives in a beautiful part of southern Utah, so I took a two-hour shuttle from the airport to meet her in St. George, Utah. Whenever my friend and I get together to visit, we always shop until we drop. When I boarded the plane in Las Vegas to come home, I looked like a pack mule. I was carrying a painting, my computer, my purse, and another bag with various home décor items that could not be stuffed into my luggage.

I was among the last to board the plane, and I was hoping and praying that I would find a spot in the upper compartments to place my painting. About a third of the way down the aisle, I looked up and was surprised to see the perfect spot available for my painting and other bag, despite the fact that every other compartment as far as I could see was stuffed. I put my painting and bag in the compartment and sat down in the aisle seat next to a woman and her daughter, and silently thanked God for His grace.

A glimpse of God at 30,000 feet

The woman hardly acknowledged me, and I managed to catch her eye long enough just to smile. About fifteen minutes into the flight, the flight attendant announced that laptop computers could now be used, so I pulled out my computer. I was working on this book.

I brought up my manuscript and was just beginning to reread some of the previous paragraphs so I could reorient myself, when the woman beside me said abruptly, "Is that about God?"

I turned to look at her. She looked apologetic. "Sorry, I was just glancing over it and it looked like it was about God."

"Yes, it is," I said.

"What is it about?"

"It's about the different facets of God's character."

"What do you mean?"

"Well, if you want to trust someone, you must first know their character. If you want to learn to trust God, you must first know His character. That's the purpose of this book."

"Oh. Do you talk about death?"

"Mmm, no."

"Do you talk about how to talk to children about death?"

"Uh, no. It's not really about that."

She told me that she was flying to be at the bedside of her father, who was rapidly dying of cancer. He wasn't expected to live through the week, and she was hoping that he would still be alive when she got there. She was a single mom who was trying to grapple with her father's death, while also trying to explain it to her five-year-old daughter.

As the flight went on, we talked about God and different parts of the book. She called herself a Christian, but didn't know much about the Bible. I asked her if she was interested in reading a few pages of the book—I thought perhaps the first chapter on the tenderness of God would be something she could use at that point. She agreed, and read the entire chapter. When she was done, she looked at me with tears in her eyes.

"Wow," she said. "I guess I knew that about God, but I had forgotten. You were supposed to sit next to me."

"I'm sure that's true," I said and smiled.

I remembered the strangely empty baggage compartment above my seat. That was so God—He gave me the perfect place for my painting—and an aisle seat—and ensured that I sat next to the one woman who needed to be reminded of His inordinate tenderness in her time of deepest need.

Thankfully, our great God of glory will not give His glory to another, so He will never be diminished in power and goodness. Yet in His amazing love and grace, He bestows glory upon us, so that through us, others are drawn to Him. When God glorifies us as believers, He fits us for a divine purpose—a purpose only we are gifted to fulfill. When we pursue that purpose, we will find ourselves accomplishing things we never could have done on our own...to show someone else a glimpse of God.

> For the Lord God is a sun and shield;
> The Lord gives grace and glory;
> No good thing does He withhold from those who walk uprightly.
> O Lord of hosts,
> How blessed is the man who trusts in Thee!
> Psalm 84:11-12

Chapter 14

Our Sovereign God

"The LORD has established His throne in the heavens;
and His sovereignty rules over all."
PSALM 103:19

God always has the last word. He will always have the decisive vote. That's what it means to be sovereign. Everything will go the way He wants it, regardless of what our wishes are. We can submit our requests to Him, and we can pray with great fervor. We can even be living in His favor—and I believe those with close, loving, daily communication with Him are—but there will always be times when He does not answer our prayers the way we want them answered. This is the rub of being a Christian.

God's sovereignty is the character trait that requires the most trust from us, because we don't always understand why He does what He does. Why does God allow bad things to happen to good people? Why does He heal some people when we ask Him, and not others? Why do some heartfelt and often-asked prayers go unanswered?

There are many scriptures that seem to tell us that if we ask, God will grant us our requests:

Ask and it shall be given to you; seek, and you shall find; knock, and it shall be opened to you.
MATTHEW 7:7

"Again I say to you, that if two of you agree on earth about anything that they may ask, it shall be done for them by My Father who is in heaven."
MATTHEW 18:19

"And all things you ask in prayer, believing, you shall receive."
MATTHEW 21:22

Believed, but not received

Many of us have followed the prescribed method of prayer. We have asked, even in the company of others and agreed upon it, and we have believed. Still, some requests have not been granted, and sometimes, even Christians wonder if Jesus' words are just a sham.

We must remember that above all, God's "will" (His plan) will be accomplished, even if it is not what we want. When Jesus first taught his disciples to pray, He taught them the Lord's Prayer. Consider how it is constructed:

Our Father, who art in heaven,
Hallowed be Thy name.

The actual term for "Father" that Jesus used was "'*abba*," "a term used by children for their earthly fathers to express the warmth and intimacy a child experiences when in the security of a loving father's care."[1] Jesus spoke to His Father with warmth and intimacy, and declared that God's name is holy. By doing that, He treated God with the highest honor.

Then He asked for two things, both relating directly to God's will.
Thy kingdom come, Thy will be done, on earth as it is in heaven.

Jesus wanted only His Father's will. Jesus knew His Father intimately, that His Father knew best, and trusted His sovereignty. Only after Jesus had begun His prayer in this way did He go on to specific requests. In essence, what He was saying was, "Father, You are My

---

[1]"Matthew." Arnold, Clinton E. Zondervan Illustrated Bible Backgrounds Commentary. Grand Rapids, MI: Zondervan, 2002.

Abba whom I know and trust, and You are holy. Therefore, I want Your perfect will for my life. Now here are my requests. If they do not align with Your perfect will, then give me what is in Your plan."

Jesus prayed in a similar way shortly before He died on the cross.

> And He went a little beyond them, and fell on His face and prayed, saying, "My Father, if it is possible, let this cup pass from Me; yet not as I will, but as Thou wilt."
> MATTHEW 26:39

The "cup" Jesus mentioned was the terrible suffering He would soon endure on the cross, and although He knew what God's will was, He did not want to go through it. Nonetheless, He knew that God's perfect will was best, even if it was going to be inordinately painful. He knew that on the other side of the suffering, there was eternal joy. Jesus was the One *"who for the joy set before Him endured the cross..."* (Hebrews 12:2)

The wonder of God's sovereignty is that, if we have given our lives over to Him, no matter what we must go through, joy is always the end result. That is His plan.

Which way to His will?

How, then, do we know what God's sovereign will is? One way is to read the Bible and to know His precepts. For example, if we wonder if God's will is to divorce or not, the Bible clearly states that God hates divorce (unless you are in physical or emotional danger). If we want to know His will in regard to a specific request, such as whether we should take a job or not, we can pray and ask Him to open or close the doors in accordance with His will, and He will do so.

Sometimes we might pray in a way we feel sure is in God's will, and yet the prayer is not answered the way we had hoped. The husband of a friend of mine moved out several months ago, after many years of marriage. My friend is a devout Christian, and she wanted to believe that through prayer, her husband would come back to her because God's will is for them to stay married. Yet her husband left with no intention of coming back, and within a few months had filed for a divorce and bought a new house. Is this God's sovereign will? No. But just because my friend's husband isn't living within God's sovereign will doesn't mean that my friend can't be. God knew long before my friend was even born that her husband would act in such a way, and He already has plans to bless her. She can't see it yet, but she has "joy set before her."

Regardless of how the world treats us, God has already anticipated it. When we ask to be in His sovereign will, we can expect joy, and for God to do "abundantly beyond all that we can ask or think." (Ephesians 3:20) It may take time for all of His plans to come together, but God will bless us.

What if I want to do it my way?

If you are not accustomed to the idea of living within God's will, it might seem on the outside to be rather limiting. "What if God's will is not *my* will for my life?" you might ask. That's a fair question. You are certainly free to live your life your way. However, that would be like the pot telling the potter how to create itself. Consider what the great potter Himself said:

> "Woe to the one who quarrels with his Maker—an earthenware vessel among the vessels of earth!
> Will the clay say to the potter, 'What are you doing?'
> Or the thing you are making say, 'He has no hands'?"
> ISAIAH 45:9

God is the potter and we are the clay. He desires to mold our lives day by day. Now, what you must determine for yourself is, do you believe He is a master artist who wants to make each vessel into a masterpiece, or simply a mass producer who makes one basic, uninspired pot after another?

The question is easily answered when you consider that every living thing that has ever graced the earth is unique. There has never been another like it. Even snowflakes are completely different. Of all the billions of snowflakes that have fallen from heaven, no two have ever been exactly alike.

God, then, is a master artist who has created you with a specific and unique will for your life, and it is marvelous. He has created you for a unique purpose, but you will only be used for this purpose if you yield to His will and sovereignty.

The right vessel for the right voyage

Let's expand upon the earthenware vessel metaphor, but let's think of you as a seafaring vessel. What if God created you to be a missionary ship ordained to reach peoples who have never heard God's truth, and who desperately need medical supplies, and yet you insist on trying to be a cruise ship because it seems so much more glamorous?

First, God will have to find another missionary ship to carry out the mission He ordained *you* for. Second, you will find over time that being a cruise ship leaves you feeling used and abused, ill-equipped and unappreciated. You would crave the quieter company of the brave missionaries you were meant to carry, and long to see the sweet, glad faces of the people they would help. This is because you weren't made to be a cruise ship, you were made to be a missionary vessel of mercy.

Now let's turn it around. What if you were created to be a glamorous, high profile cruise ship, ordained to transport the rich and influential to remote and exotic places—places so distant from their self-absorbed lives that God would have a chance to speak to their hearts and actually be heard—yet you felt you couldn't possibly be glamorous enough to measure up to their standards, and therefore decided to become a missionary ship to avoid the possibility of failure? Your life would become drudgery as a humble missionary ship because you were made to be around lots of people, music, chatter and activity. Deep in your soul, you feel the emptiness inside many wealthy people, and you have a heart that longs to help them, to be the one God uses to bring them to His heavenly shores.

Would God accomplish His purposes if you don't choose to be the vessel He designed you to be? Yes, but you would miss out on the joy of playing your unique part in His wonderful plan.

When your ship comes in

God created us for a specific purpose. It's in our DNA. That purpose is always tied to His sovereign will, but the wonderful thing about it is, once you find your purpose, you find JOY. In my writing career, I have written an enormous amount of stuff, including a fiction book, children's books, newspaper and magazine articles, and two screenplays. Although some of my magazine and newspaper articles were published, I found it was a struggle to write these things and to get them published, even though I had a college degree in journalism and knew without a doubt that I was a writer. Some of this is part and parcel of the writing profession, but it just didn't seem to be clicking.

Then, in my late forties, as I began to write this book under what I felt was God's direction, this unfamiliar feeling began to bubble up within me. It wasn't earth-shattering, but it felt something like…joy and accomplishment and *arrival*. I had finally arrived at my port (better late than never), the port of call for my particular vessel!

If we bow to God's sovereign will, we will not be limited; we will be unleashed and supernaturally equipped to do the only thing that will give us joy. So how do we find out what God's sovereign will is for our lives? We must simply ask Him.

> "Ask and it shall be given to you; seek, and you shall find; knock, and it shall be opened to you.
>
> "For everyone who asks receives, and he who seeks finds, and to him who knocks it shall be opened.
>
> "Or what man is there among you, when his son shall ask him for a loaf, will give him a stone?
>
> "Or if he shall ask for a fish, he will not give him a snake, will he?
>
> "If you then, being evil, know how to give good gifts to your children, how much more shall your Father who is in heaven give what is good to those who ask Him!"
>
> MATTHEW 7:7-11

God wants us to have a life of deep fulfillment. His plan for our lives is more exciting and more meaningful than anything we could ever imagine for ourselves. Remember, He is *God*. Following is one of my favorite portions of scripture:

> Now to Him who is able to do exceedingly abundantly beyond all that we ask or think, according to the power that works within us, to Him be the glory in the church and in Christ Jesus to all generations forever and ever. Amen.
>
> EPHESIANS 3:20-21

God is able to do *exceedingly abundantly beyond all that we ask or think*. That means way beyond what we could ever imagine. So, do you want what you think you want, or do you want what He wants to do with your life?

Timing is everything

Once we ask Him, we may not get an immediate answer. This is another aspect of God's sovereignty which is irrefutable: His timing. We usually want things right now, but quite often, it doesn't happen that way. God answers us at the right time, the perfect time, the *appointed* time:

> There is an appointed time for everything. And there is a time for every event under heaven...
>
> ECCLESIASTES 3:1

Answers to prayer cannot come fast enough for us. When it seems nothing is forthcoming, we feel like we're praying into empty space. But God has the big picture, and He is weaving many lives together to bless not just us, but people we may not even know. When we do not receive answers to our prayers, or God does not answer them in the way we had hoped He would, it is not because He doesn't care about our wishes. It's that He has something better in mind, or a specific plan which our request does not fit into.

A few years ago, my husband and I wanted to put some money into real estate. We didn't have much money at the time so I went online to see what we could get for a fairly small amount down, and small payments. This narrowed the field considerably. My good friend who is also our realtor went out with me to look at a few cottages that were for sale on the coast of Washington, about an hour from where we live.

We found a very tiny cottage, located directly above a bay, with a beautiful view. It had a fabulous deck that perched above the water, and we were in love. In fact, my realtor friend fell in love with it, too, and we talked about buying it together. I wasn't sure about buying it together—my friend is wonderful, but I didn't know how the usage of the cottage would work between our two families—but splitting the payment looked very attractive.

However, after we paid an inspector to check out the cottage, we found that it had serious structural problems that would need to be corrected. We would have considered putting the money into the cottage except for the fact that it was located on leased land, so we would be buying the structure only, not the land. Since the structure really wasn't the outstanding aspect of the property—the land was—we began to feel uncomfortable about the deal.

My realtor, my husband and I backed out of the cottage deal, and you know the rest of the story. About a year later, my grandmother passed away, and we were able with our inheritance to buy our wonderful cabin in the woods—the one that God tailor-made for us, wrapped up and tied with a bow.

Only He could see that cabin waiting there for us. Only He knew that we would soon be able to afford a bigger, more wonderful cabin on our own. It is the same with all of our requests to God. He may not give us what we want because He wants to give us something better.

Are we there yet?

Waiting for answers to prayer is perhaps the most difficult part of the Christian walk. I do not always endure the waiting in a saintly fashion. Several months ago, I awoke at 3:30 a.m., and could not get back to sleep. I got a cup of hot chocolate and my Bible and trundled up to the bonus room, where I can pray aloud in the middle of the night and feel relatively assured that I will not be overheard. Many of the sentences in my monologue began with, "Why....? When....? I'm tired of ...." Then I capped it off with the petulant, "If You don't have any intention of having this book published, and You're not going to use the writing talent You've given me, and I'm just going to end up living a life of complete mediocrity, then, would You please prepare my heart?" (I live with two drama queens. It has either rubbed off, or they inherited it from me. Surely it's the former.)

When you've given your life to the Living God—and have given up control of your destiny—it can seem like you're spending a lot of time looking up into heaven with a big question mark in your eyes. That's because waiting is a big part of being a Christian—waiting for God to answer prayer, or to give us direction in our lives.

We can take comfort in knowing that if we have given our lives to Him, He is always acting in our behalf.

> For from of old they have not heard nor perceived by ear,
> Neither has the eye seen a God besides Thee,
> **Who acts in behalf of the one who waits for Him.**
> ISAIAH 64:4

Because we know He loves us, and we are the apple of His eye, we can trust in His sovereignty. We can trust in His timing. And we can experience joy right now, knowing that He is going to bless us abundantly, beyond all that we ask or think.

Chapter 15

Our Romantic God

The LORD did not set His love on you nor choose you because you were more in number than any of the peoples, for you were the fewest of all peoples, but because the LORD loved you...

DEUTERONOMY 7:7-8A

Deep in the heart of every human being is the knowledge of the kind of love they were made for. That knowledge was put there by God, and it is, in fact, every person's true heart's desire. It is no less a desire of men than it is of women.

Little boys look for that kind of love from their mothers, but as they grow older, they look for it in women. However, this is where men often lose touch with their heart's desire, because they confuse their hormones and sexual drive for the love that their soul craves. They try to satisfy their soul's inner longing with sex, but find that the satisfaction of sex is only temporary, and still leaves their soul's love needs unmet.

This is not to say that men and women weren't designed for beautiful sexual relationships within marriage. But sex was not designed to meet that inner need for the perfect love of God. The need for God's love is an entirely different need, and one that everyone longs for, but many can't figure out how to meet.

As little girls grow up, they look to both their mother and their father to meet their need for that perfect love, and eventually, in men. Even though girls turn into women, they still secretly look for their Prince Charming, even after they are married. This is because their husbands weren't designed to meet that need.

The love of God is the kind of love that our soul longs for, and God, in the form of His Son, Jesus Christ, is the only true Prince Charming. Every woman, regardless of age, knows in the depths of her heart what He is like, even though she has never met Him face-to-face. He is what she craves, what she longs for. When she says, "I want someone who will treat me right," she is actually saying, "I want God's perfect love." She *knows* that He is kind, thoughtful, compassionate, attentive, gentle yet strong, authoritative, faithful, generous, protective. She *knows* that He knows her inside and out, all the good and the bad, and still loves her with a sacrificial love. She *knows* that He's seen her looking her worst, yet still sees her as inordinately beautiful. Even women who do not acknowledge God know what true love is like. They could describe it. It's because we were made with the longing, and God is the answer to that longing.

It's something like the way that God designed man and woman for lovemaking. The man was designed to fit inside the woman and for the two to become one. Similarly, we were designed to be made complete in the love of God, and for His love to perfectly fill that empty place in our soul.

While we can experience that love relationship with God now as *"seeing in a mirror dimly,"* (1 Cor. 13:12) when we are finally face to face with Him, we will have our innermost longing fulfilled. As Paul puts it, then *"we shall know fully just as we also have been fully known."* God has fully known us all along, but then, we shall know Him fully, and we will be completely and wholly and eternally satisfied.

Of course, our relationship with God is not sexual in nature, and that's why men as well as women crave His love. Many men have managed to suppress this God-given longing, since it doesn't really fit into the persona they are expected to grow into. *They* are expected to be the strong ones, the leaders, and also the pursuers and protectors of women. So why is it, they wonder, that deep in their soul, they want Someone who is stronger, wiser, more authoritative, and able to protect *them*, and to pursue *them* with relentless love? It doesn't jive with society's mores, and so they don't want to acknowledge it, but in fact, that's precisely what they were made for.

Looking for His love in all the wrong places

Women do not suppress the longing for God's perfect love, but instead, try to get their husbands to supply it—to be their Prince Charming—but they are utterly incapable. This is no dig toward men; women are similarly incapable of being Princess Charmings. Many women try to find this Prince Charming, and go through man after man, and eventually become embittered because eventually each man, no matter how hard he tries to fit the mold, becomes what he truly is: human. In fact, it's only when we finally release our husbands and wives from being our God, the beloved of our souls, do we take an enormous amount of tension out of our relationships.

Only God can supply us with perfect love. Only God knows what we need exactly when we need it. Only God can woo us and captivate us eternally with His own brand of romance. Only God knows how to love us the way we desperately desire to be loved. Only God knows our own individual love languages, and can speak them to us, and delight us with His personalized affection.

"You are Mine!" Sigh...

God is the quintessential lover. I can't help but sigh with pleasure when He declares His possessiveness and protectiveness toward us:

> "Do not fear, for I have redeemed you; I have called you by name; you are Mine! When you pass through the waters, I will be with you; And through the rivers, they will not overflow you. When you walk through the fire, you will not be scorched, Nor will the flame burn you. For I am the LORD your God, The Holy One of Israel, your Savior; I have given Egypt as your ransom, Cush and Seba in your place."
> ISAIAH 43:1B-3

I have given Egypt as your ransom. This sounds like something that would issue from the mouth of Omar Sharif in *Lawrence of Arabia*, except that Omar Sharif is merely an actor, and no person in history has been able or even willing to give the huge country of Egypt for anyone's ransom. But these were not mere words from God. He actually meant them, and true to His character, He did as He said:

> The Lord rewarded Cyrus the Persian Monarch for liberating them [the Israelites], by permitting him and his son Cambyses to possess Egypt and the neighbouring kingdoms. Seba was the large district between the White and the Blue Nile, contiguous to Ethiopia. The possession of these lands was not merely a gift, it was a ransom price (a kopher, or covering), the people on whose behalf payment was made, being covered by it.[1]

God is all that Omar Sharif never was. Let's look at His declaration in Isaiah again:

"I have called you by name. You are Mine!"

In this text, the word "called" comes from the Hebrew word, "*qârâ,*" which means, "to cry out, to call aloud, to roar; to proclaim, to pronounce, to preach; to call, to summon." Once you see His words in this context, you realize that God is not in the least bit timid about His love for us. He *roars* out our names, and proclaims in no uncertain terms, YOU ARE MINE! I love the exclamation point. There is absolutely nothing passive about God. He is nothing if not passionate. Can you not help but fall in love with this lion of a God?

God actually describes Himself as a lion in many passages in the Bible. *"A lion has roared! Who will not fear? The Lord God has spoken!"* (Amos 3:8) Even Jesus is described in Revelation as the Lion from the tribe of Judah. (Rev. 5:5)

---

[1]MacDonald, William. "Isaiah." Farstad, Art, ed. <u>Believer's Bible Commentary,</u> (quoting Vine, W. E. <u>Isaiah—Prophecies, Promises, Warnings.</u> London: Oliphants, Ltd., 1947). Nashville, TN: Thomas Nelson Publishers, 1995.

There is something thrilling about being loved by a lion-like God. When you know that your heavenly Father is big, has a loud roar and very sharp teeth, you realize that there is nothing to fear, nothing at all. If you find yourself in an uncomfortable or unsafe situation, just imagine the Lion by your side. He is there, as close as the hairs on the back of your hand. He will protect you, because He loves you and He promises it in His word:

> He who dwells in the shelter of the Most High
> Will abide in the shadow of the Almighty.
> I will say to the Lord, "My refuge and my fortress,
> My God in whom I trust!"
> For it is He who delivers you from the snare of the trapper,
> And from the deadly pestilence…
> You will not be afraid of the terror by night,
> Or of the arrow that flies by day;
> Of the pestilence that stalks in darkness,
> Or of the destruction that lays waste at noon.
> A thousand may fall at your side,
> And ten thousand at your right hand;
> But it shall not approach you.
> PSALM 91:1-3, 5-7

When I was in my early twenties, I rented out the basement of a house that was within a few blocks of the beach in southern California. I worked full time, and sometimes would go down to the beach in the evenings, and walk along the sand. I loved the darkness and the roar of the waves, because I could talk to God aloud without feeling self-conscious.

I was rarely completely alone because there were always other people walking along the beach. Nonetheless, when my mother, who lived in another state, heard that I was walking on the beach at night, her heart nearly stopped. She cautioned me that someone could attack me and no one would hear my cries. But I was never afraid, because I knew I had a lion of a God by my side.

While I don't advocate walking along the beach alone at night, my God knew that I wasn't doing it simply to put Him to the test. Living in a crowded beach town, I was faced with people everywhere I went. The only place I could go to be alone was the tiny little basement that I rented out—and the beach at night. The feel of the wind on my face was like His tender caress, and the beauty of the wild, luminous waves made His presence palpable. I knew He understood that I needed those walks with Him.

When we go out to meet God, He is already waiting for us. *God waits for us.* That wonderfully absurd concept never fails to amaze me. Shouldn't we be the ones waiting to gain an audience with *Him?* Yet He is the one who waits for us to come to Him; *longs* for us to come to Him:

> Therefore the LORD longs to be gracious to you,
> And therefore He waits on high to have compassion on you.
> For the LORD is a God of justice;
> How blessed are all those who long for Him.
> ISAIAH 30:18

What this means is that God wants to lavish us with His incredible love and favor, but He does not waste His blessings on those who don't want them anyway. He does not throw His pearls before swine (Matt. 7:6). Yet those who long for Him as He longs for us are the most blessed people on the face of the planet. The more we run to Him, the more He comes to us and reveals Himself to us, and grants us His favor.

He speaks our love language

God's love is very individual. God does not have a blanket love for everyone, although many people in the world choose to believe it. We are not cookie-cutter people to God, not little gingerbread men who look the same and are treated the same. God loves us as individuals and treats us as individuals, and we are blessed according to the devotion and trust we give to Him.

The more we strive to get to know Him—what's known in the Bible as "seeking His face"—the more He will strive to show us Himself. He will meet us more than halfway, and always in our own particular love language. He knows how to show us in our lives that He is there—and even how to communicate with us—particularly when we are open to it.

Recently, He showed me He loved me by answering a small desire in my heart that I hadn't even voiced to Him. Through a series of unfortunate events, my baby pictures were lost. When my own children came along, I was sad that I had absolutely no pictures of me as a baby to show to them.

Out of the blue, my great aunt, whom I haven't seen in years, sent me two pictures, one of me as a toddler, and one of me as a baby. As I gazed down at the picture of me as a baby, the tears welled in my eyes, because I knew that my great God had seen the desire that had been tucked deep in the darkest recesses of my heart, and blessed me with two pictures. This is how God speaks to us in our own individual love languages.

I have a girlfriend who, at 45, is a brand new Christian. She often calls to tell me how God speaks to her in her own specific love language. The numbers "720" are significant in my friend's life, because July 20 is her birth date, and she seems to see those numbers everywhere.

My friend had a mastectomy about a year ago, and has since been trying to find a doctor who will do reconstructive surgery. Due to her insurance, she is limited to a small number of doctors. She saw one particular doctor a few months ago, and he was not encouraging. She left his office in tears. When she could find no one else who had the same expertise as this doctor, she decided to try him again. At her second visit, her husband dropped her off, and then drove the few blocks to his work. My friend was preparing herself for the worst, and felt agitated and nervous. When she sat down in the waiting room, she did some deep breathing to help herself calm down, and said a prayer, asking God to help her.

To her surprise, when she met with the doctor, he was far more encouraging, and they talked about how they could do the kind of surgery that would make her feel like a whole woman again. When she left his office, she was all smiles as she walked the few blocks to her husband's work. It was a beautiful sunny day in Seattle, and just as it occurred to her that perhaps God had answered her prayer, she glanced up to see an address on the side of the building she was passing. The numbers "720" were emblazoned on a large, golden address plate that was shining brilliantly in the rays of the sun. She knew instantly that God had raised her head to see those numbers at that moment, and that He was saying to her, "Yes, I heard you, beloved, and I have been with you. I love you."

This is the kind of individual attention God lavishes on those who love Him, and seek His face. Those who don't seek God and strive to serve Him miss out on the most amazing romance of their lives. God's absolute attention is on those who love Him, and He never takes His eyes off of us.

> "For the eyes of the LORD move to and fro throughout the earth that He may strongly support those whose heart is completely His."
>
> 2 CHRONICLES 16:9A

Note the key word in the verse above: *completely.* God wants us to love Him with all of our heart, our soul and our might. And if this should seem the least bit demanding, isn't this what you would want from a husband or wife? Or would you settle for just a feeling of fondness between the two of you? Certainly some people do, but God is not in any way a lukewarm lover. Consider what Jesus said to the church of Laodicea:

> "I know your deeds, that you are neither cold nor hot; I would that you were cold or hot.
>
> "So because you are lukewarm, and neither hot nor cold, I will spit you out of My mouth."
>
> REV. 3:15-16

The Laodiceans were very wealthy due to the production of a fine quality of famous glossy black wool, and a huge banking industry. They were complacent, self-satisfied and indifferent to the real issues of faith in Him and of discipleship.[2] They were merely giving Jesus lip service, but God detests an attitude of compromise. Either our hearts burn with love for Him, or they are cold as ice. Those who want to play it safe and stay on middle ground are actually living very dangerously.

As stated elsewhere in this book, there is a clear difference in the way God looks at and treats those who reject Him and those who love Him. Those who reject Him are treated as disposable. Those who love Him are treated with royal deference. This may come as a shock to some, but God is no fool:

> "Since you are precious in My sight, Since you are honored and I love you, I will give other men in your place and other peoples in exchange for your life."
>
> ISAIAH 43:4

This is God the king speaking, who extends the royal scepter to those whom He loves and highly esteems. Can you imagine standing in the massive throne room of heaven, gazing at the all-powerful King of Kings sitting on His throne, and being told that you are precious in His sight, that you are honored, and that He, the majestic, omnipotent One, loves you? That He would give other peoples' lives for yours? Has anyone else ever made you feel so cherished?

He wants nothing less than all of you

God wants to be loved as wholeheartedly as He loves us. In God's amazing, sacrificial love for us, He has withheld nothing—not even His most beloved Son, the darling of heaven—and He expects our complete love, trust and devotion in return. Of course, He knows our

---

[2]Barker, Kenneth L. and John R. Kohlenberger III. "Revelation." The Expositor's Bible Commentary. Grand Rapids, MI: Zondervan, 1994.

limitations and doesn't expect us to meet him toe-to-toe. He doesn't expect perfection, but He desires that we love Him with everything we've got.

> "And you shall love the LORD your God with all your
> heart and with all your soul and with all your might."
> DEUTERONOMY 6:5

What God is really asking for is *relationship*. He wants to share our lives with us. He wants us to talk about our desires, hopes and dreams with Him, so that He can help us to bring them to life. Did it ever occur to you that God placed desires in your heart so that He could fulfill those desires for you? If you had no desires, hopes or dreams, how could He bless you? If you are the person who has everything, how could God show His love for you?

He wants to be part of everything you do. Why would someone who loves you build a house for you, just so that you can live alone in it? Why would someone who adores you put you in a job that keeps you so busy that you rarely see him after that? What is the good of any good thing, without someone to share it with? God knows that only when He is involved with you, can you have true joy in the accomplishment of your life's purpose. And it brings Him joy to help you to fulfill your dreams.

I was walking one evening several months ago, and having a conversation with God. Deep in my spirit, I heard God say, "So what are your dreams?" I had to smile. "You really want to know?" I said. Of course He already knows what they are, but He wanted me to bring them out and take a look at them. Some were so far back in the dark corners that I'd forgotten they were there. So I began to dig deep, and think about all the things I really wanted in life. I talked about the things I hoped for in the future, things like good health into old age, companionship in my marriage, the ability to watch our children marry and have their own children, having a book published, speaking about my great God in front of an audience, and maybe even a log cabin by a stream.

By the time I arrived home, my eyes were sparkling. God and I had had a great conversation. I realized that I hadn't always talked to God about some of them, because I was afraid if I dug some of them out of the dark and overlooked corners of my soul, and held them up to Him and asked for them, that He would say "no" and I would be disappointed. So I'd kept them hidden away, out of harm's reach. I knew if I didn't ask for them, I'd never get a "no." But then again, I'd never get a "yes" either.

But God, the lover of my soul, cares about the things in those dark corners, just like my longing for the baby picture. When He started prodding in my heart, I gingerly pulled out a few of them. "Well, um, after the book is published—if it is, you know—I might like to speak in front of women's groups. I don't know if I'd be very good, but I want to tell them how amazing You are."

I sensed God's nod of encouragement.

"And…I've always wanted to live in a log cabin in the country. But Robin, my husband, has the kind of job that usually requires a city, so, I understand, Father, if that doesn't happen…"

Within a month of this conversation with God, I drove to meet my friend and her husband in the town of Sandpoint, Idaho. They live in Utah and I live in Washington. My friend Terry doesn't fly anywhere, and doesn't like to drive long distances, either, so whenever she comes my direction, her husband usually drives her. So, the three of us converged on Sandpoint, Idaho. Terry's husband Ralph had just retired from the fire department, and they wanted to look at the town to see if it would be a place they might like to live. We spent a day looking at real estate, and late in the day, we drove up to a wonderful log house.

The three of us looked at each other, and before they could say a word, I hissed teasingly, "You can't have it. It's mine." We all walked in and fell in love. It had a natural pond in the backyard, was situated on eight acres, and was the log cabin of my dreams. It had been on the market for nearly a year.

Ask Him already!

When I came back home and plopped myself down in my prayer chair, I was afraid to ask God for it. All the potential roadblocks to having the log cabin were in front of me:

a. It was six hours away; if we bought it, would the distance become an annoyance?
b. How often would we be able to go over there and enjoy it?
c. Robin's career in the software industry would never enable us to live there because it is located in a small town.

But then, the Lord prodded me gently. "Hey, I'm God, remember? Why are you afraid to ask Me? Don't you know I'm the one who took you on that trip, and showed you that log house? Don't you realize I know what's in your heart, and don't you think I, your beloved, want to give it to you?"

That log cabin is now ours, a testament to our amazing God, the great romantic.

God's one desire

God has a desire in His heart, too—a desire that cannot be met until we die. We are His beloved and He wants to be with us, not just in spirit, but in body, *up close and personal*. He wants to dwell among us, just as Jesus did. He wants to be the One who personally dries the tears from our eyes, with real hands. He wants to draw water from the spring of the water of life and offer it to us. He wants us to see His face. (Rev. 21:3-22:4) He has loved us from afar because sin has separated us, but like any lover, He wants eye-to-eye contact. Can you imagine looking into the eyes of God?

God did not create us so that He could love us from afar. He created us so that we could be together with Him, in actual physical contact. So when we long for that perfect love deep in our souls, it's because we long for that perfect lover, Who also longs for us! We aren't longing for a love relationship with a spirit we can't see or touch. Although God is omnipresent and Spirit (the Holy Spirit), God is also Someone we can recognize as a person. He has the appearance of a man, with hands (Ezekiel 8:2-3, Rev. 5:1), feet (Exodus 24:10), eyes (2 Chron.

16:9), arms (Deut. 33:27) and breath (Gen. 2:7). He created us with the same characteristics so that we could hug each other, touch each other, and look into each others' eyes.

Even now He longs for us to hear His real voice and His wonderful laughter. He wants to tell us how much He loves us, how beautiful we are, and how prized. He longs to show us Himself, just as a lover longs to be in the physical presence of his beloved. He has watched us and loved us from afar, but oh, how He longs to be able to touch us with physical touch, and for us to hear Him in clear sentences. We are not the only ones waiting for our ultimate Lover; He waits and longs for us, too.

Until that time comes, know that He is in your midst, loving you as only our Great Romantic can do. If you have not yet given Him your whole heart, there is no time to waste. It doesn't matter what you've done in your life; what sins you've committed. All can be cleansed and forgiven by asking God's Son Jesus to come into your life as Lord and Savior.

Life is short, eternity is long and the chasm between heaven and hell is unbreachable. You wouldn't want to find yourself on the wrong side now that you know how wonderful God is.

If you've never prayed the prayer to accept Jesus Christ as Lord and Savior, it's easy. Just bow your head, and say these words: "Lord Jesus, I am a sinner, and I ask you to come into my life, forgive my sins, and be my Lord and Savior. Thank you for dying for me and for giving me the gift of eternal life. Amen."

To order additional copies of

God, Up Close and Personal

have your credit card ready and call
From USA: (800) 917-BOOK (2665)
From Canada: (877) 855-6732

or e-mail
orders@selahbooks.com

or order online at
www.selahbooks.com

LaVergne, TN USA
27 April 2010
180723LV00003B/9/P

9 781589 302457